The Reminiscences

of

Vice Admiral Charles A. Pownall

U.S. Navy (Retired)

Copyright © 1989
U.S. Naval Institute
Annapolis, Maryland

# Preface

The Naval Institute's oral history program began 20 years ago, in 1969. One of the individuals interviewed during the first year of the program was Vice Admiral Charles A. Pownall, U. S. Navy (Retired). In the statement that follows this preface, Admiral Pownall's daughter explains why the transcript was not released earlier and why she has now agreed to release it.

Admiral Pownall's name shows up in history books primarily because of his command of the fast carrier task force at the beginning of the Central Pacific campaign in World War II, and he covers that experience in the transcript that follows. But that tour of duty was only part of a naval career that spanned some four decades. He describes in addition such things as his World War I destroyer experience, going through flight training as a mid-level officer, serving in the commissioning crews of the carriers Saratoga (CV-3) and Ranger (CV-4), and commanding the famous Enterprise (CV-6). While ashore he served in the Bureau of Aeronautics, commanded the naval air station at Norfolk, commanded the training establishment that turned out thousands of wartime naval aviators at Pensacola, and capped his career by serving as Governor of Guam and High Commissioner of the Pacific Trust Territories.

The interviews were conducted for the Naval Institute by Commander Etta-Belle Kitchen, U. S. Navy (Retired). The smooth typing of the transcript was done by Ms. Joanne Patmore and the indexing by Ms. Susan Sweeney, both of the Naval Institute's oral history staff.

                                        Paul Stillwell
                                        Director of Oral History
                                        U. S. Naval Institute
                                        March 1989

## Statement of Explanation

After listening to the tapes and having read the transcripts, I feel compelled to make a few statements in the preface by way of explanation. At first I was reluctant to release them at all, but I realize that that would be unfair to my parents as well as to future historians. My reluctance was based on the fact that at the time of the interview my father was 83 and had just recovered from a severe illness (a condition which later worsened and finally led to his death). The hesitation, uncertainty and lack of an organized presentation which he shows in the interview were not in any way characteristic of my father as an active duty naval officer. Actually he was always well organized and had a very strong and decisive personality.

In defense of my mother who appears to be interfering unnecessarily, I wish to say that she was very concerned about his health and skeptical about his being strong enough physically to participate in the interview.

At the time I had a job and so was not present during any of the interviews, but I do recall hearing my parents discussing what approach they would take. Since my father was known for his talent as a raconteur and had been urged by his classmates to write some of his more amusing sea experiences, my mother advised him to concentrate on those stories rather than getting involved in some of the more serious aspects of his career. Also my father had a very high code of ethics and definite scruples about talking behind a person's back or after his death. Since some of his critics had no such restraints, I wish he had been a little more candid in answering Commander Kitchen's questions.

Despite the fact that the interview does not give a true picture of Charles Alan Pownall, the naval officer, it does paint a picture of our Navy and the events during his lifetime.

                              Louisa Pownall Wagner
                              (Mrs. Robert L. Wagner)
                              Daughter of Vice Admiral C.A. Pownall

21 September 1988

VICE ADMIRAL CHARLES ALAN POWNALL, U.S. NAVY (RETIRED)

Charles Alan Pownall was born in Atglen, Pennsylvania, 4 October 1887, son of Dr. Howard W. Pownall and Mrs. Hannah Louisa Walter Pownall. He attended public schools in Altoona, Pennsylvania, and Mount Hermon (Massachusetts) School (class of 1908) before his appointment to the United States Naval Academy, Annapolis, Maryland from the 19th District of Pennsylvania in 1906. While a midshipman he won class numerals in fencing, and was manager of the fencing team as a first classman. He was graduated on 3 June 1910, and served the two years then required by law before being commissioned ensign. Thereafter he advanced in grade as follows: lieutenant (junior grade), May 1915; lieutenant, 1 July 1917; lieutenant commander, 1 July 1918; lieutenant commander, 3 June 1921; commander, 1 July 1930; captain to rank from 23 June 1939; rear admiral, retroactive to 3 December 1941. His transfer to the retired list of the Navy became effective 1 November 1949, when he was advanced to the rank of vice admiral on the basis of combat awards.

Upon detachment from the Naval Academy in 1910, he had consecutive duty in the USS Mississippi (BB-23), the USS Missouri (BB-11), and the USS Ammen (DD-35) until April 1914. He then joined the USS Reid and was given temporary command of that vessel, which was assisting in convoying General Funston's army to Veracruz, Mexico. The Reid also participated in the subsequent bombardment and the American occupation of that city. In April 1915 he reported to the Navy Yard, Norfolk, Virginia, for duty in connection with fitting out the USS Aylwin and served aboard that destroyer from her commissioning 25 May 1915. In September 1915, he returned to the U. S. Naval Academy Postgraduate School for instruction in steam engineering, continued the course at Columbia University, New York, New York, and received the degree of master of science in 1917 from that university.

From March 1917 until January 1918, he served as executive officer of the USS Roe (DD-24), transferring to command of the USS Vedette (SP-163). Returning to the Roe as commanding officer, he served from June to August 1918. He was awarded the Navy Cross and cited "For distinguished service in the line of his profession as Commanding Officer of the USS VEDETTE and later of the USS ROE, engaged in the important, exacting, and hazardous duty of patrolling waters infested with enemy submarines and mines, in escorting and protecting vitally important convoys of troops and supplies through these waters, and in offensive and defensive action, vigorously and unremittingly prosecuted against all forms of enemy naval activity."

In August 1918, he reported as aide on the staff of Commander Naval Forces Europe. On 30 January 1919, he arrived home and reporting to the Navy Department, Washington, D.C., he was assigned duty in the Material Division, Office of the Chief of Naval Operations.

Ordered to the Asiatic Station in July 1921, he assumed command of the USS John D. Ford (DD-228) at Cavite, Philippine Islands. Relieved of command of that destroyer in May 1923, he joined the staff of Commander in Chief Asiatic Fleet aboard the USS Huron (CA-9) as aide, fleet operations officer, and fleet athletics officer.

When detached from the Asiatic Fleet in September 1924, he returned to the Navy Department, Bureau of Engineering, and served in the Ship Repair Division. In July 1925 he was assigned duty as aide to the Assistant Secretary of the Navy, and after one year he reported for flight training at the Naval Air Station, Pensacola, Florida. Designated a naval aviator on 30 March 1927, he remained at Pensacola until the following August, when he reported for fitting out duty in the USS Saratoga (CV-3), building at the American Brown Boveri Electric Corporation, Camden, New Jersey. Commissioned on 16 November 1927, he reported aboard as navigator and in December 1928 he transferred to the USS Lexington (CV-2) as air officer.

He joined the staff of Commander in Chief Battle Fleet in November 1929 as aide and fleet aviation officer, USS California (BB-44), flagship. From May to August 1930 he was attached to the staff of Commander Aircraft Squadrons Battle Fleet, USS Saratoga, flagship. Returning to the Navy Department, he reported for duty in the Bureau of Aeronautics, and for three years served as head of the Power Plant and Experimental Section. In August 1933 he assisted in fitting out the USS Ranger at the Newport News Shipbuilding and Dry Dock Company, Newport News, Virginia, and served as her executive officer from her commissioning on 4 June 1934 until June 1936.

For one year he had duty as chief of staff and aide to the Commander Aircraft Base Force and then returned to the Navy Department, Bureau of Aeronautics, to serve as head of the flight division until December 1938. He commanded the USS Enterprise (CV-6) from December 1938 until March 1941, at that time assuming command of the Naval Air Station, Naval Operating Base, Norfolk, Virginia.

In May 1942, he was designated Commander Patrol Plane Replacement Squadrons, Patrol Wings, Pacific Fleet, and was later assigned duty as Commander Fleet Air, West Coast.

From August 1943 to January 1944, he commanded Carrier Division Three and organized and commanded Task Force 15, attack force on Marcus Island, Gilbert Islands, and Tarawa, and later the Carrier Task Force 50, occupation and defense force. For services in that command, he received a letter of commendation with ribbon from the Commander in Chief Pacific Fleet, and the Distinguished Service Medal. He also received the ribbon for and facsimile of the Presidential Unit Citation awarded the USS *Yorktown* (CV-10). The citations follow:

Letter of Commendation: "A carrier striking force under your command executed an air attack on Marcus Island on September 1, 1943. The highly satisfactory results of this attack have been fully attested by photographs taken during the course of the action. I have reviewed the statement of intentions and the detailed plans which you prepared for this operation...This was an essential preface to so fine a success...."

Distinguished Service Medal: "For exceptionally meritorious and distinguished service to the Government of the United States in a duty of great responsibility as Task Force Commander of the Central Pacific Force during the seizure and occupation of the Gilbert Islands in November and later as Commander of the Task Force which raided the Marshall Islands in December, 1943. . . Maintaining control of the air throughout the entire period, he later directed vigorous attacks against enemy aircraft, shipping and shore emplacements, which culminated in the successful completion of each hazardous assignment. . ."

Presidential Unit Citation--USS *Yorktown*: "For extraordinary heroism in action against enemy Japanese forces in the air, at sea, and on shore in the Pacific War Area from August 31, 1943, to August 15, 1945. Spearheading our concentrated carrier-warfare in forward areas, the YORKTOWN and her air groups struck crushing blows toward annihilating the enemy's fighting strength; . . Daring and dependable in combat [she] with her gallant officers and men rendered loyal service in achieving the ultimate defeat of the Japanese Empire."

Following temporary duty with the Commander in Chief Pacific Fleet, Vice Admiral Pownall was ordered, in February 1944, to duty as Commander Air Force Pacific Fleet. Upon his return to the United States he reported, in September 1944, for duty as Chief of the Naval Air Training Command, Pensacola, Florida, and was also assigned additional duty as Chief Naval Air Intermediate Training Command, and Commander Naval Air Training Base, Corpus Christi, Texas. For this service he was awarded the Legion of Merit and cited: "For exceptionally meritorious conduct

. . . from September 9, 1944 to August 31, 1945. Displaying the highest order of leadership, initiative, foresight, sound planning and administrative ability [he] directed the vast and complicated training organization under his command in delivering to the Fleet approximately 14,000 trained Naval Aviators and 24,000 trained Combat Aircrewmen who, by their performance in combat against the enemy in all theatres of the war against the Axis, have passed on to the service of the Navy and the Nation the results of his inspired leadership and devotion to duty. . ."

In February 1946, he assumed duty as Commander Marianas, and on 7 May 1946, with the approval of the President, the Secretary of the Navy directed that he reestablish the naval government of Guam, and thereafter he served as Naval Governor of Guam. Ordered relieved of that assignment, he was detached in September 1949. The following month he reported to the office of the Chief of Naval Operations, Navy Department, and was thereafter relieved of active duty pending his retirement on 1 November 1949.

In addition to the Navy Cross, the Distinguished Service Medal, the Legion of Merit, the Commendation Ribbon, and the Presidential Unit Citation Ribbon (USS Yorktown), Vice Admiral Pownall has the Navy Expeditionary Medal; Mexican Service Medal; Victory Medal with Destroyer Clasp; American Defense Service Medal, Fleet Clasp; the Asiatic-Pacific Campaign Medal; the American Campaign Medal; and the World War II Victory Medal. He was also awarded the Distinguished Service Order by the government of Great Britain, for "outstanding gallantry and leadership" in the Gilbert Island campaign.

He was married in 1912 to Mary Ellen Chenoweth of Altoona, Pennsylvania. Their daughter is Louisa Pownall Wagner. Admiral Pownall died 19 July 1975 at San Diego, California.

Authorization

The U.S. Naval Institute is hereby authorized to make available to libraries, other repositories, and individuals of its choosing the transcripts of two oral history interviews concerning the life and career of the late Vice Admiral Charles A. Pownall, U.S. Navy (Retired). The interviews were recorded with Vice Admiral and Mrs. Pownall on 11 April 1970 and 12 April 1970, in collaboration with Commander Etta-Belle Kitchen, a representative of the U.S. Naval Institute.

During the lifetime of the undersigned, permission must be obtained from the undersigned prior to quoting or citing in any published work material from the tape recordings or transcripts of the interviews. The copyright of both the oral and transcribed versions shall be the sole property of the U.S. Naval Institute. The tape recordings of the interviews are and will remain the property of the U.S. Naval Institute.

Signed and sealed this 22nd day of August 1988.

Louisa Pownall Wagner
Mrs. Robert L. Wagner
(for the estate of Charles A. Pownall)

Pownall #1 - 1

Interview Number 1 with Vice Admiral Charles A. Pownall,
U.S. Navy (Retired), and Mrs. Mary Pownall

Place: The Pownalls' home in La Jolla, California

Date: Saturday, 11 April 1970

Interviewer: Commander Etta-Belle Kitchen,
U.S. Navy (Retired)


Q: Good morning, Admiral, I'm glad to see you and you're looking so well. When I came in I said, "How are you?" and you said you were old. I must confess that if you're old it makes it seem a charming experience.

Do you want to begin by telling me when you were born, which is a good way to begin?

Admiral Pownall: October 4, 1887, I was born in Atglen, Pennsylvania, and grew up in the schools there. There came a time when the school teacher asked me to write an essay on Admiral George Dewey.* That was my first introduction to the Navy.

Q: Did she pick him out, or did you?

Admiral Pownall: She did. She said, "Charles, your assignment is George Dewey." I didn't know much about the Navy until that time.

---
*Admiral of the Navy George Dewey, USN, hero of the Battle of Manila Bay in May 1898 and president of the Navy's General Board from 1900 until his death in 1917.

I'd been in the League Island Navy Yard in Philadelphia.* My father took me there once. I was earmarked to be a doctor, I think, like my father was.

I wrote the essay. My friend's father was the judge of Blair County. When I went out there that night for dinner, I started to tell them all what I knew about George Dewey. The old judge said, "Charles, do you want to go to the Naval Academy? If you do, come in the study after supper."

So I went in the study after supper, and he gave me a letter. I took it to the hotel, Logan House, in Altoona and gave it to a congressman.

I went away to school, and while I was away at school, I received a telegram from my father, "You've received an appointment to the Naval Academy. I know nothing about it." That's how I got into the Navy.

Q: An interesting beginning. It's interesting so many people have so many different experiences and ways in which they did get into the Navy.

Do you have any reminiscences of your young days or your family that you feel influenced you in becoming the kind of person you are?

Admiral Pownall: I always had a good mother. Not

---
*Later known as the Philadelphia Navy Yard and now as the Philadelphia Naval Shipyard.

particularly, I just had a normal life of a youngster.

I went to the Naval Academy. I was manager of the fencing team, and I was in love.

Q: With the Navy, or with somebody?

Admiral Pownall: With Mrs. Pownall; she was my gal then.*

Q: Where did she come from?

Admiral Pownall: The same town. We grew up together.

Q: Did you really? Isn't that lovely. A while ago you said, "I'm an old Quaker."

Admiral Pownall: Yes. I'm an old hexite from that part of Pennsylvania. I was born in Atglen, and that's Quaker country.

When I finally got this appointment, my mother said, "Well, if it's all right with thee, it's all right with God."

---
*Then Miss Mary Ellen Chenoweth of Altoona, Pennsylvania. The couple was married in 1912.

Q: That was a strong influence in your life, wasn't it?

Admiral Pownall: Yes. And I resigned once from Quaker meeting.

I was in Washington on duty there; a lot of this non-preparedness stuff was out. I couldn't stand for that as a naval officer, and I sent in my resignation as a Quaker.

I received a reply back, "Dear Charles, thy request to resign is declined. If thee believes in preparedness, thee prepare. But do not hold thy religious brethren in contempt who may have opposite ideas."

Q: That was a proper view really, wasn't it?

Admiral Pownall: Yes.

Q: That's interesting. I've never known a Quaker before. I guess Mr. Nixon's a Quaker, isn't he?*

Admiral Pownall: He was. I don't know if he still is.

General Butler in the Marine Corps was a hexite

---

*Richard M. Nixon was President of the United States when the interview was conducted.

Quaker, from Chester, Pennsylvania.*

Q: I should say I haven't had the occasion to interview a Quaker before.

Admiral Pownall: I remember General Shepherd here in town said, "Oh, Pownall, you're a Quaker.** We had a couple of good Quakers in the Marine Corps. General Butler was one.

Q: Do you still follow the Quaker teachings?

Admiral Pownall: I haven't given it up. I tried to resign and was declined, so I'm still a Quaker. I'm a friend of the Presbyterian Church. I take my sweetie there.

Q: What is her first name?

Admiral Pownall: Mary Chenoweth Pownall.

Q: I must say that she is a beautiful lady.

So what are your recollections from the Academy?

---

*Major General Smedley D. Butler, USMC, a native of West Chester, Pennsylvania. After being involved in U. S. military intervention in the Caribbean, Central America, and the Far East through the 1920s, Butler embraced the peace movement in the 1930s.
**General Lemuel C. Shepherd, Jr., USMC (Ret.), Commandant of the Marine Corps, 1952-55.

Admiral Pownall: I didn't stand too well in studies. I was interested in this fencing team. When I was a senior, I made a trip to New York to change their rules. We won the trophy that year against the Army and Cornell and a few others. But it was a little hard on my class standing. I was about in the middle.

Q: That's all right. That looks as though you had a well-rounded career, that you were not completely devoted to any one thing.

Admiral Pownall: Mrs. Pownall is in the Lucky Bag.* She was the girl with the sprawly handwriting.

Q: Admiral Pownall is showing me his picture in the Lucky Bag. This is 1910, the year you graduated. In it, it refers to him as a class married man.

Why don't you read that first sentence? I think that's very interesting.

Admiral Pownall: Pownall: "Good old Baldy! The class married man and the recipient, thrice daily, of the letter with the sprawly handwriting." That was Mary.

"A serious-minded man with a big heart and an earnest disposition that leads him to work with all there is in him

---
*Lucky Bag is the name of the Naval Academy yearbook.

at any labor he may have set for himself."

Q: That's a nice statement. I think your career will prove that to be true.

Admiral Pownall: Thank you.

It ends, "Mr. Pownall, who threw the mince pie in your face?"

Q: Do you want to tell me what that means?

Admiral Pownall: I don't remember it.

But I was a "clean-minded, whole-souled, openhearted man."

Q: Oh, who threw that mince pie in your face?

Admiral Pownall: Skip Merrill, captain of the fencing team, threw a pie in my face.* We were having an argument. It was for fun.

Q: So your recollections of your Academy days are extremely pleasant, I guess.

Admiral Pownall: Yes, true.

---
*Midshipman Robert T. Merrill II, USN, also a member of the class of 1910.

Q: And you graduated in the class of 1910. How soon were you married?

Admiral Pownall: I was graduated as a passed midshipman. And I didn't marry until 1912.

Q: I think you could explain that a little bit.

Admiral Pownall: Later they graduated as ensigns, and they could marry right away. But in my day, you had to graduate as a passed midshipman.* You were two years a passed midshipman, then you were made an ensign, and then you could marry.

Q: So you were married in 1912.

Do you want to tell me about your early service in the Navy?

Admiral Pownall: Yes, I would to this extent--I'll tell about my first boner.

I graduated and went to the USS Mississippi. We went to Gravesend, England. I was a young passed midshipman and

---

*The term referred to the fact that a midshipman had "passed" the four-year Naval Academy course. After two years of sea duty, he was then given additional exams and commissioned as an ensign.

a junior officer. I was sent ashore at Gravesend to a rugby game with the enlisted men and a band. We were entertained quite nicely. Sir Gilbert Parker was there and so on.* They should have sent a more senior man than a passed midshipman in charge of it, but they didn't.

The bandmaster came to me and said that he had permission from the officer of the deck for the band to go on liberty direct. They didn't have to go back to the ship. I was inexperienced and took his word for it. I took the instruments and went back to the ship with the liberty party. The first thing, the officer of the deck said, "Where's the band?"

I said, "They said they had permission to go on liberty."

"Like hell, they're due on the flagship tomorrow morning at 8:00 o'clock. You see the executive officer."

I went to see Wat Cluverius, one of the finest men.** He had just been made exec. He said, "You know, the band has to be on the flagship tomorrow morning. So, Pownall, the only thing I can recommend is that you go ashore and get the band in Gravesend [on a Saturday night]. I'll give you two good enlisted men to help you get that band, but you get the band. I won't tell the captain, unless you don't get the band."

---
*Parker was a British novelist and member of Parliament. In 1914-15, he directed the British publicity effort in the United States.
**Commander Wat T. Cluverius, USN.

I resurrected the baritone horn blower on top of a tram car with his arm around a girl. She was mad, and so was he. But I got them all except one, but he was on liberty. The two enlisted men and myself got the band back aboard.

About 3:00 o'clock in the morning I rapped on the exec's door and said, "We're back."

He said, "Thank you, well done. We'll handle the bandmaster at mast tomorrow. Good night."

Q: The bandmaster had lied to you?

Admiral Pownall: Yes. He got a little drunk, I think. The English half and half was a little strong for him, I guess. I should have known that, but I was too inexperienced.

Q: You were just a youngster, really.

Admiral Pownall: Yes, I was. So that was my first boner.

Then the other thing was Sims.* Our great Commander Sims was an expert on gunnery. At that time, the Navy at 2,000 yards couldn't hit the side of a barn door. In fact, they couldn't hit the barn itself, so they used to say.

---

*In March 1909, despite his junior rank, Commander William S. Sims took command of the USS Minnesota (BB-22).

Pownall #1 - 11

Sims changed that.

He was given command of the Minnesota. He was only a commander. He was designated to go to Guildhall and represent the commander in chief of the fleet at a Guildhall luncheon. I was assigned as one of his aides.

He said, on the way up on the train from Gravesend to London, "I wonder if I have to make a speech." Then he went off by himself to a corner of the coach. When he got to London, he didn't have anything written, but he had it up here. He made the famous speech, "Blood is thicker than water."*

Q: Do you remember any more of it than that?

Admiral Pownall: No, I just remember that. I lost my hat, I remember, waving applause.

Q: Who all was at the luncheon?

Admiral Pownall: Every captain of the various ships was there. And Sims was there also. He was the one that was designated to make the speech. The English ships were there, too.

---
*Sims made the speech on 2 December 1910. A description of the event is in Elting E. Morison, Admiral Sims and the Modern American Navy (Boston: Houghton Mifflin Company, 1942), pages 277-280.

Pownall #1 - 12

Q: All of the skippers of the English and American ships were there?

Admiral Pownall: Yes, yes. The speech was objected to by the Kaiser. Sims was detached soon after that, and he was relieved of his command.

Q: Where was the luncheon? Do you remember?

Admiral Pownall: The luncheon was in Guildhall in London. We were at Gravesend, about 15 miles down the River Thames. Then we went to Brest, France.

The class of 1910 had me write a couple of yarns.

Q: Maybe you'll let me have a copy to attach to your biography.

Admiral Pownall: Okay. Here is one of the yarns:

"In the summer of 1910 we sailed for Europe. Imagine the consternation when at sea en route to Brest, France, the Idaho [that was the ship along with us] reported that a very low person or persons unknown had stolen their race boat. Also the future consternation that arose when it was finally discovered to be resting serenely on the boat skids of her principal rival, the USS Mississippi. [I was on the

Mississippi.]

"Investigation that would have done credit to the FBI followed immediately, proving that the Mississippi had been so original and bold as to succeed in swapping two race boats.

"Meanwhile, the Mississippi had been thrown into great sorrow. Our hero Hyde, who died of pneumonia, his body in a sealed casket, was stored on the boat skids adjacent to the famous race boat awaiting the ship's return to a U. S. port.

"Reader, you guess the correct answer to the mystery. Yes, Hyde was labeled as the guilty one.

"Now comes to the front the high sense of sportsmanship which exists between ships in the fleet, then and now. The Idaho race boat's crew petitioned that Hyde's name be cleared and further that the boat be invoiced to the USS Mississippi for keeps--this in honor of Hyde."

Q: Had he really been the one who had stolen it?

Admiral Pownall: Yes. He was the coxswain of the race boat. The ships are tied up together and the boats are put in the water. The Idaho had all the money in the fleet, because they had the best boat. The Mississippi had the worse boat, and were poor. Old Hyde was captain of the race boat. He wanted to change all that. If he could get that good boat into the Mississippi, we'd make a little on races. You know, we always bet on races. That's the story.

Q: But he did die?

Admiral Pownall: Oh yes, he died of pneumonia.

To go on with the story--when I went aboard the Mississippi, you had to get in full dress uniform. We had a very tough exec. He ordered my friend and I into the race boat end of the collier right away, right in our good clothes. This was hazing.

We went in and were coaling. Then we were allowed to go change into dungarees, but not before a guy wire took my good brand-new cap and threw it into the Delaware River. Old Hyde jumped in after it. That was my introduction to Hyde.

Q: Must have been quite a young fellow.

Admiral Pownall: Yes, he was. He got pneumonia. I don't know whether jumping into the Delaware River after my cap was responsible for it or not, but he died of pneumonia very soon afterwards.

Those were my initial stories as a passed midshipman.

I went from the Mississippi to the Missouri.

Admiral Nimitz then had submarines on the Castine.* These were the big fleet submarines. Nimitz invited me over to have lunch. He was a commander then. He wanted to interest me in submarines.

I went back and wrote a request to go into submarines. Chapin was my captain, but I was a spotter.** Spotters were not available to transfer to submarines, so I didn't get into the submarines, but I tried to.

Q: The Institute is writing a biography of Admiral Nimitz.*** Do you recall his appearance, what he said, what he did, anything that would be of interest to the biographer relating to Admiral Nimitz? Do you remember what he was like? He would have been quite a young man then.

Admiral Pownall: Yes, he was full of business.

We had his apartment when we were in Washington. But that's another story.

Q: We'll tell about that. You won't forget it, will you?

I wondered how he impressed you when he was a young naval officer.

---
*Lieutenant Chester W. Nimitz, USN; The USS Castine was a gunboat which served as a submarine tender from 1908 to 1913.
**Captain Frederick L. Chapin, USN.
***The biography, titled Nimitz, was written by E. B. Potter and published by the Naval Institute Press in 1976.

Admiral Pownall: Very much.

Q: Would you otherwise have gone into submarines, if your skipper had approved it?

Admiral Pownall: Yes. The skipper, Chapin, was a very fine man.

It happened also, while I was on the Missouri, that some Cubans had taken a sugar mill back in Guantanamo that was built by Americans and owned by Americans. This made our President, Taft, mad.* The Marines were busy in Nicaragua, but that didn't faze our President. He ordered the commander in chief to form a battalion of bluejackets and go ashore at Guantanamo, and capture that sugar mill and return it to its lawful owners.**

Q: That's an incident in history that I don't know about.

Admiral Pownall: I was the signal officer on the Missouri and also the aide. I was made adjutant of this battalion, because our captain was the junior captain in the fleet.

So we dyed our white uniforms in coffee to go ashore as a battalion. When we were all ready, after drilling at

---
*William Howard Taft, President from 1909 to 1913.
**This incident took place in June 1912.

Guantanamo, we went ashore with the band playing and walked up to the mill.

Meanwhile, my skipper said, "Fix bayonets." I had trained these kids, but I wasn't so sure about the bayonets, whether they'd do more harm to them or to the Cubans. They did. The upshot of it was one dead Cuban, and he was killed by another Cuban.

That was one of these Cuban incidents. It was settled with one loss of life and that by a Cuban, and with a battalion of bluejackets with Captain Chapin commanding.

In spite of all the troubles we had in Cuba at that time, we used positive action and straightened it all out.

Q: How many men did you have?

Admiral Pownall: Four companies; it was a modified battalion.

Q: What did you do with the sugar mill, once you had recaptured it?

Admiral Pownall: Gave it back to the owners, and they started up the business again, as far as I remember now. We went back to the ship.

Q: That was typical of the approach that our government

Pownall #1 - 18

took in those days; they used the Navy personnel.

Admiral Pownall: Soon after that, I was detached from the Missouri and ordered to a destroyer, the USS Ammen. I went aboard and had the duty that night. It was in Newport, Rhode Island. A storm came up, and we dragged all the way across Newport Harbor. So I certainly was indoctrinated in shiphandling.

Later, Charlie Belknap relieved Jim Allen.* Belknap was a very wonderful man.

About that time, I met Sims again. They put the reserve destroyers back in commission and ordered officers to command them. It happened that on the Reid, the man that was supposed to take command was taken sick. Sims, who was in command of the destroyers then, inspected the Reid, and he didn't like things aboard and he detached the commanding officer on the spot--I won't mention his name-- and put one of his staff officers in command.** Half of the crew was drunk. He had a big boat come alongside--the Birmingham's boat--and take the drunks off.

Q: Aboard ship?

---
*Lieutenant William H. Allen, USN; Lieutenant Charles Belknap, Jr., USN.
**Captain William S. Sims, USN, Commander Atlantic Destroyer Flotilla from 1913 to 1915. His flagship was the cruiser Birmingham.

Admiral Pownall: Yes, they were drunk on the _Reid_, approximately half of them.

Then I was innocently back on the _Ammen_. I was chief engineer of the _Ammen_. Then the captain called me in and said, "You're to command the _Reid_." I was an ensign, three years out of the Naval Academy. The _Reid_ was a nice, big ship, a destroyer. I didn't have any officers.

This is interesting--when I was ordered to go over and command the _Reid_, I asked first if they'd give me my drunks back. I said, "I think I can cure them."

But Sims said, "No, I won't do that."

I knew I wouldn't get the smack of the destroyer squadrons with the replacements. You don't transfer your best men.

Belknap said, "You're going to take three or four men of your own, because you may have a problem over there on the _Reid_." So I took the chief water tender, the chief machinist's mate, and the chief electrician. They all had good right arms, and were well brought up. So we went over to man the _Reid_.

Q: As an ensign you were given commanding officer?

Admiral Pownall: Yes, at Veracruz. That's the time of the Funston's Brigade.*

---
*Brigadier General Frederick Funston, USA, landed with a brigade at Veracruz, Mexico, on 30 April 1914 to relieve the naval forces which had gone ashore there on 21 April.

Q: I want to get to that in a minute, but I was so interested in your experience on the Reid as an ensign commanding officer.

Admiral Pownall: I didn't have any officers. All I had was chief petty officers.

Q: How did you make out? Can you tell me something about that?

Admiral Pownall: Yes, they were fine. I slept on the bridge.
   Then, when we got to Veracruz, they realized that we were violating the steamship rules by sending a ship to sea with only one officer, so they gave me the damndest . . .

Q: I just never heard of that before. I think that's fascinating.

Admiral Pownall: I had to put him under hack in Charleston. I had to put my own man that I ate my meals with under hack.

Q: What had he done?

Admiral Pownall: He got drunk and stayed ashore all night, when he should have been back.

Q: Your only officer deserted you under this crisis. What was his name?

Admiral Pownall: I won't say. I know he's dead now.

Q: Who did you say was skipper of the Reid, who was relieved?

Admiral Pownall: I won't tell you that. I have no gripes. It's a matter of history.

Q: I wanted to hear about your trip down to Veracruz.

Admiral Pownall: This ship, the Reid, was certainly shot. Her bottom blows, the boiler, one fireroom, leaked. Fortunately, the convoy duty only required one fireroom. But we had to shift coal from one fireroom over to the other over the deck. It was terrible. The condensers were gone; everything was just shot. How I ever got her down there, I don't know. But she did; she hung together.

When we got back, we went to Charleston Navy Yard and

she was repaired. Then we went on neutrality duty up in Boston.

Q: Can you tell me something about the experiences in Veracruz that you had?

Admiral Pownall: Yes. I can say that we got the transports into Veracruz. I wanted to get the ship so I could wash her out. She was salted up. It happened that my ex-instructor in languages at the Naval Academy was a three- or four-striper, and he was the chief of staff to Admiral Fletcher.* I went to him. He said, "You're salted up?"

I said, "Yes."

He said, "You should be court-martialed."

Then on my way back to my ship, some Mexican took a shot at me, but I got behind a pole and finally got back. I don't like Veracruz. Mary's trying to get me to go to Mexico, but I don't know that I'm in any hurry to go back to Mexico.

Q: Do you want to put on the tape something of the background of why the ships were going to Veracruz?

---

*In April 1914, Rear Admiral Frank Friday Fletcher, USN, Commander First Division, Atlantic Fleet, directed the landings at Veracruz.

Admiral Pownall: I don't know that part of it. The British and the American ships were in Veracruz. I was so busy with my little old Reid that I don't remember much about that.*

Q: You were so busy keeping your ship afloat and your people aboard that you probably didn't know. Did any of the people on your ship take part in any action down there?

Admiral Pownall: Oh, yes. They landed. My ship did not, but others did. The transports did, with a brigade of soldiers. Before that, other American naval ships had landed their own landing force, but the USS Reid did not. We were late getting there, and I didn't land any men, wasn't ordered to. Of course, I tried to fix up the ship.

One thing I will say about Sims, God bless him. I called on him at Veracruz, and he returned the call in all his regalia, which was a nice gesture.

One other thing that may have happened on the way down. My good chief water tender, Kluge--she didn't have any air locks and this boiler let go, and they had to pull the fires right out into the fireroom. This funny man, he was supposed to be a chief. I'll never forgive the people that sent him to me. He started to open a hatch, and had he opened the hatch he would have killed every man in that

---
*For a full account, see Jack Sweetman, The Landing at Veracruz: 1914 (Annapolis: U. S. Naval Institute, 1968).

fireroom. I made a lunge, and Kluge made a lunge. Kluge got there first with a 24-inch monkey wrench.

I said to myself, "Gee whiz, you're captain of this ship. So you better get out of here and get back of a boiler, because you may have to give this man a court-martial." But Kluge got there and he saved it.

Q: Was he trying to get out?

Admiral Pownall: No, he was trying to open the hatch.

Q: To get out?

Admiral Pownall: No, he didn't understand. With the boiler gone, had he opened the hatch--he thought it was air locked, but it wasn't air locked. The old <u>Reid</u> had one, but it didn't work very well.

Q: What would have happened, if he'd opened the hatch?

Admiral Pownall: All the fire would have gone out into the fireroom. It would have hurt those men.

Q: That's an experience to remember, isn't it?
That explains an item I was going to ask you about--

Pownall #1 - 25

where it says you had a temporary command, so that was on the Reid, of course. How long did that last?

Admiral Pownall: It lasted a couple of years. I went to Veracruz, then went to neutrality duty in Boston in 1914.

Q: And what does that mean?

Admiral Pownall: When war was on, we were protecting--then I went to another destroyer. The man who was originally ordered to command came and took his ship at the Boston Navy Yard. I went on the Aylwin. I was slated to go to postgraduate school. So from there I went to the Aylwin for a short time, and then to the postgraduate school at Annapolis. Our daughter was born in Annapolis. I had one year at postgraduate and then a year at Columbia.

Q: Where you got your master's degree.

Admiral Pownall: Yes.

Q: Did we cover the neutrality duty? How long were you in Boston before you went down to Norfolk?

Admiral Pownall: About a year in Boston.

Pownall #1 - 26

Q: What were your duties there?

Admiral Pownall: To protect American shipping against submarines and so forth. We were to convoy American ships on the high seas out to so far out to sea.

Then I went to postgraduate school, and after Columbia the war broke out.

I went to sea as exec of a destroyer, the Roe. We convoyed out to Europe, from New York and Boston.

Q: Can you tell me some detail about that, because I know you received the Navy Cross for your work? I'd love to have you tell me of the incidents or the experiences that you can remember from those two duties. Then you became the commanding officer of the Vedette.

Admiral Pownall: Yes. I was exec of the Roe. Then went to the Vedette as the commanding officer. We were on Brittany patrol, running from Brest to La Pallice, on the coast of Spain, under a French admiral.*

Q: It sounds like you'd have lots of interesting things to tell, so I'm just going to sit and listen and let you regale me with all your experiences during those years.

---
*La Pallice is on the coast of France where it adjoins the Bay of Biscay.

Pownall #1 - 27

Admiral Pownall: Let me get my memory working again. I'm doing this all without notes.

Q: I think it's just remarkable.

Admiral Pownall: I remember that the Roe, in the first convoy across, salted up her boilers because we had ferrule condensers. Barnes was my captain, and he said that he could make repairs if he was on this towline for not more than eight hours.* A cruiser was sent back to take us in tow.

Then the admiral, Gleaves, got worried about the transports.** We were convoying transports to Europe. He said, "Cut the towline." Here we were in the middle of the Atlantic. They cut the towline, and here was this poor dinky destroyer--I was exec of this destroyer; I never felt so lonesome in my life--rolling her insides out and they had to fix the condenser before we got back to port. The orders were to, "Make your best way to the United States." We were all alone. We got into St. Johns, Newfoundland. From St. Johns, Newfoundland, we finally got into Boston. But that was some experience.

Q: What time of year was it?

_____
*Lieutenant Guy Carlton Barnes, USN.
**Rear Admiral Albert Gleaves, USN, Commander Atlantic Fleet Cruiser and Transport Force.

Admiral Pownall: It was in the fall of the year.

Q: Fortunately, it wasn't in the wintertime.

Admiral Pownall: No, it wasn't.

We were convoying, and then one or two times later, there seemed to be oil out there in the middle of the ocean at longitude 13. The destroyers had come back to New York.

From the convoy--the Queenstown destroyers would take over the transports and take them either to Queenstown or Brest. We went two-thirds of the way and then turned around and oiled from a tanker. This time, a destroyer had hit the tanker, and there wasn't any oil. So we got into Brest. Sims had been trying to get more ships over there to fight the war, and kept us.*

I served then on the Vedette on the French coast from Brest to La Pallice under a French admiral. We had about two knots better than the ships we were transporting, so we were not very effective, but we were pretty good. I was on the Vedette. Then my skipper on the Roe was taken sick, and I was ordered to command the Roe. This is interesting--the Roe was ordered to Liverpool for a refit. My orders were to stop at Queenstown and pick up Sir Lewis Bayly, the admiral commanding the British forces in

---

*In May 1917 Sims was promoted to vice admiral, and the following month his title was changed to Commander U. S. Naval Forces Operating in European Waters.

Queenstown, Ireland.*

It got foggy then, and I intercepted this message from the British, HMS <u>Hollyhock</u>, "Lying to off Daunt light vessel, harassed by fog."

I said, "Well, I can't use that language in the American message." But I finally found the light vessel and picked up Sir Lewis.

He said, "Pownall, I have to be in Liverpool at 8:00 o'clock tomorrow morning. I see it's a little foggy, but don't you think you can do it?"

I said, "Yes, sir."

I gave him my cabin down below. We hit the Irish Sea at 25 knots in a dense fog. I was on the bridge the whole time. We got into Liverpool, into Mersey River, where I anchored.

I had a nice clean gig. Sir Lewis came down, saluted, shook hands, got in the gig, and said, "Well done." I'll never forget him.

He used to come over to New York with the British. We had the Queenstown Association, and he and his niece would come. Sims would be there and very nicely invited me, too.

Q: I'm sure he never forgot that trip.

Admiral Pownall: We got there at 8:00 o'clock.

Another thing about Sir Lewis--in front of his desk was

---
*Vice Admiral Sir Lewis Bayly, RN.

a little rug about two feet by a foot. When you were told to stand on the rug, you knew you were going to catch something or other, or a commendation. Because it was the rug for officers reporting to Sir Lewis.

McKittrick--old Mac is dead now--had touched his ship at Hollyhead and had to go in dry dock.* He was up before Sir Lewis on the rug, shaking. He thought he was going to lose his command or something. McKittrick described the fact that on a certain morning his ship had touched a rock off Hollyhead. Sir Lewis said, "That's singular. That's the first rock I hit." I think it's a good story.

Q: It's a good story, and saved him, I'm sure.

Let me read what the Navy Cross says. May I refresh your memory? The citation is as follows:

"For distinguished service in the line of his profession as commanding officer of the USS Vedette and later of the USS Roe, engaged in the important, exacting, and hazardous duty of patrolling waters infested with enemy submarines and mines, in escorting and protecting vitally important convoys of troops and supplies through these waters and in offensive and defensive action, vigorously and unremittingly prosecuted against all forms of enemy naval activity."

---
*Lieutenant Harold V. McKittrick, USN.

Admiral Pownall: The Vedette was Frederick Vanderbilt's yacht.* She could make 13 knots, which was pretty good for an old, small yacht.

This is, I guess, interesting enough--I was the junior one in that escort. We were going to Penmarch. We used to lose a ship practically every night. We finally got the French to change the running of Penmarch to daytime, instead of night, so we could have a chance.

Q: Will you explain what you mean by that?

Admiral Pownall: We couldn't see at night and all of a sudden one ship would be torpedoed. In a foggy dark night, we didn't have much of a chance in fog and darkness. If we went in the daytime, we could see what we were doing.

I went back to the Roe command out there on the Bay of Biscay escorting. All of a sudden we saw a submarine on the surface. Believe it or not, our ship, the Roe, hit that on the first shot off the bow. It was just plain luck and we got credit for it.

Soon after that, I was put on the staff at London. I thought certainly that I'd be assistant chief of staff, at least. Instead of that, I was assigned to the secretarial section.

_____
*Frederick W. Vanderbilt was a New York financier and philanthropist.

Q: What was your job there?

Admiral Pownall: Personnel and transportation under Sims.

Admiral Stark was flag secretary.* He's a wonderful man, still is. He's in Washington.

So I went on Sims's staff then.

Q: Did you have more than the one contact with enemy submarines?

Admiral Pownall: No. Of course, they were around you all the time, but this was off Brest when we actually got a hit. In the convoy you never see them, but this time we did. He was on the surface. To me it was the only time I ever engaged a submarine.

Q: I know they don't give the Navy Cross lightly, so I know that you may not be describing the things that you did and saw and participated in in as much detail as they deserve.

Admiral Pownall: You're not supposed to. I'm not going to toot my horn.

---
*Lieutenant Harold R. Stark, USN, later Chief of Naval Operations from 1939 to 1942.

Q: I don't expect you to think of it in that way, but again I want it for the interest of someone listening to this.

Don't cheat them of interesting things.

Admiral Pownall: As the citation says--that's a very good citation, in there that--habitually employed in fighting so and so and so and so and so and so. And we were. Every time you went to sea, you were subjected to harassments that way.

Q: It says--"engaged in important, exacting, and hazardous duty of patrolling waters infested with enemy submarines and mines, and protecting vitally important convoys of troops and supplies."

Admiral Pownall: That's just about it. The fellow that wrote that had it right.

Q: I may have interrupted your chain of thought when you were speaking of the French and your having them change their operations order to go in the daytime instead of night. Was there more that you wanted to tell on that?

Admiral Pownall: One time, I picked up a crew of a French

cruiser that was torpedoed. Also an American ship, the <u>Westward Ho</u>, was torpedoed. And I picked up the crew of the <u>Westward Ho</u>. We had them in the firerooms. You have a full crew yourself and then take on another crew on a destroyer; it's something.

Tahitians were in this other ship. I should have saved one of those and taken him along with me. Because when we got back to Brest, the Frenchmen came aboard and said, "Have you any French subjects aboard?"

I said, "No." Had I saved one, I'd have gotten a Croix de Guerre.

John Halligan, our chief of staff at Brest, was a very fine man.* I later served under him as his navigator on the <u>Saratoga</u>.

They were pushing out all these Legion of Merits and so forth. An officer asked John, (I happened to be there and heard it.) "Do you have anything in the United States to compare with the Legion of Honor?"

John saw all these medals being passed out, everybody under the sun on the list. John said, "Yes."

"What is it?"

"The Elks."

"Oh, I never heard of them."

I don't think that will hurt the French, will it?

---
*Lieutenant Commander John Halligan, Jr., USN.

Q: No, that won't hurt the French a bit.

At this point I don't think we're interested in your biography as it hurts or harms anybody, only as it affected you and what things happened that interested you.

Admiral Pownall: Now we're at Brest. There were a lot of nice people in Brest. Emil Bart was a French captain. He had two or three daughters, and he lost a son. It was nice for us to be able to go to his house on liberty, and he'd give us something to eat. Old Emil was a very patriotic Frenchman. He told me, "You know, I give half my income to France, not including my Russian holdings. I certainly wouldn't give them that." His Russian holdings weren't worth very much, but he gave half his income.

Elaine and Marie were both nurses in a French hospital, and some hospital, too. The surgeon kept the instruments in a bureau drawer. Our hospitals just got along with what they could, because we had it and they didn't, but we soon made sure that they did have it.

Q: I'm sure you saw a lot of heroism and a lot of bravery during those years on the ships that were performing that duty.

Admiral Pownall: I don't remember much of those exact episodes. We had good crew; we had good personnel.

Pownall #1 - 36

Q: What was your reaction or your feeling when you knew that you had sunk a German submarine?

Admiral Pownall: I wasn't elated.

Q: Because you knew they were human beings, despite the fact they were the enemy.

Admiral Pownall: I'd rather fight them on the surface where you could see them.

Q: Do you have any anecdotes of the time you spent in London when you were aide to the staff of Naval Forces Europe in London? Have you told me who the Commander of Naval Forces was then?

Admiral Pownall: Sims. I had personnel and transportation.

These fellows at sea, when they'd come in, I was in the outer office, and I'd take their orders and so forth. One was old Cap Bemis, who just died the other day.* It was in Shipmate.

I remember Cap when he came in. He'd been down in Bantry Bay south of Ireland with the submarines; he hadn't seen any females for I don't know how long. He came in and had to write a report to Admiral Sims. He sat down and tried to think. I had this Miss Reagen. I commanded two stenographers; one was Mrs. Nash and the other Miss Reagan. Miss Reagan was a very beautiful gal.

I would see old Cap looking at Miss Reagan and try to write. Then he'd look at Miss Reagan and try to write and finally he said, "Oh, I'll do it in longhand."

I didn't drink tea. Mrs. Nash said, "You're over here in England and you must drink tea." So she'd come in my office and put up a pot of tea and an American and British flag and say, "It's tea time now."

That was a good staff over there. Stark is a fine man. He's still alive. Twining was our chief of staff to Sims.*

Q: The air general?

Admiral Pownall: No, there's a lot of Twinings.

This chief of staff Nathan Twining was Chief of the Bureau of Ordnance, a naval officer. This other Nathan was his nephew, with the same name.**

I lived at Hans Crescent Hotel. I heard somebody mention it the other day. I said, "I used to live at the Hans Crescent."

He said, "Well, it's still going, off Knightsbridge."

You'd get a bucket of coal to try to keep warm, a little bit of hard coal, Cardiff coal.

---
*Captain Nathan C. Twining, USN.
**General Nathan F. Twining, USAF, was Chief of Staff, U. S. Air Force, 1953-57, and Chairman of the Joint Chiefs of Staff, 1957-60.

Pownall #1 - 38

Q: Mrs. Pownall was with you?

Admiral Pownall: No, no, we couldn't have any gals over there.

Q: Then where were you when the war ended?

Admiral Pownall: I was detached and brought a lot of papers back with me, and reported to the Navy Department. I came back to the United States and was in the Bureau of Material Division of the Office of Chief of Naval Operations.

Q: You were in Washington then for a couple of years with CNO.

Admiral Pownall: Yes, that's right. Nimitz was there also. He had the submarines, Charley Blakely had the destroyers, and I had what was left.*

Q: What does that mean?

Admiral Pownall: Tugs and yachts and so forth.
One amusing thing--the _Vedette_ had been owned by

_____
*Commander Charles A. Blakely, USN.

Frederick Vanderbilt, and when war was over the Vedette went back to Frederick Vanderbilt. He said that everything was fine, except he'd like to know the blankety blank that had taken out that staircase in his yacht. It was mahogany, and I had to do it to make a compartment.

So the Chief of Naval Operations said, "Pownall, you're just in a fine position to answer this letter." So I told him it was wartime and we had to make room. The other thing was the machinist's mate of the engine room had a room off the engine room. Before it had been the maid's room; it was in pink tapestry or something. The old chief couldn't stand that, he wanted a can of war paint. So the maid's room ended up in war paint.

Q: I know that Mrs. Pownall was with you that time in Washington, for those two years.

Admiral Pownall: Yes. I'm trying to think where we lived. Mary, where did we live in Washington then?

Mrs. Pownall: We lived in the Ontario and rented Admiral Hughes's apartment.* His father-in-law was the great Admiral Clark.** He took a brand-new ship all away around

---
*Rear Admiral Charles F. Hughes, USN, later Chief of Naval Operations, 1927-30.
**Rear Admiral Charles E. Clark, USN. As a captain in 1898, Clark was commanding officer of the USS Oregon.

Cape Horn and went into the Battle of Santiago. They called him "Oregon Clark" because he took the Oregon, which was brand-new.

Admiral Pownall: I'll have to tell a little story on her. Admiral Clark liked to play bridge, and Mrs. Pownall plays bridge, so he would get ahold of her to fill in with the chum club.

Mrs. Pownall: There were five of them. One of them was an old colonel of the Confederacy. I forget who the others were. Practically every week one of them would be sick, so they would ask me to substitute. I wish I could remember all the stories they told me about their wives and so forth. It was wonderful.

Admiral Pownall: I'll tell a story, too. We had Admiral Hughes's furniture.

Q: You rented Admiral Nimitz's place later on, didn't you?

Mrs. Pownall: It's the same. Admiral Nimitz was living in it first. He was the one that told my husband about it, but it was Admiral Hughes's apartment. It was his furniture.

Pownall #1 - 41

Admiral Pownall: It was his furniture. Now I'll get to my story--Mary was telling Admiral Clark that. And Admiral Clark said, "Do you mean to say that you pay Freddie [Hughes] for this damn stuff, for this furniture? You should charge him for storage." So we could never get a bill out of Admiral Hughes after that, so we had furniture for nothing.

Mrs. Pownall: We were all very young then. My Charles had been made a temporary lieutenant commander after the war.

Q: So you were young in Washington in the spring.

Do you have any more recollections of that period in Washington?

Mrs. Pownall: I don't think there was anything particular that was very outstanding. You were working very hard.

Admiral Pownall: Yes. I don't see anything around here that reminds me.

Q: You did become a lieutenant commander during that period, which was quite an event in those days. Do you want to move on then to your next duty on the Ford?

Admiral Pownall: Yes. Then I was ordered to sea on the

<u>John D. Ford</u>, practically a brand-new destroyer, built by the Cramp Shipbuilding Company.

I'll tell you something before that--Sims came out that our ships should not deteriorate, particularly destroyers. He had to defend his statements, he said, "Lessons of the war." And he wrote the lessons and one thing was we ought to learn how to keep destroyers in good material condition. That made the Secretary of the Navy a little mad.

Sims had to prepare a statement, and he wanted some papers out of the Navy Department. Of course, I was in the Navy Department then. I couldn't take them without making sure that Coontz would approve.* Coontz was Chief of Naval Operations.

So I went to him and said that Admiral Sims needed some data. Then I said, "I can't take it."

Coontz said, "Confidential files of the Chief of Naval Operations are open to any officer in good standing, and I consider Sims as in good standing."

Q: So you were able to get him what he wanted.

Admiral Pownall: I think this speaks well of Coontz.

Q: You took command of the <u>Ford</u> at Cavite, didn't you?

---
*Admiral Robert E. Coontz, USN, was CNO from 1919 to 1923.

Pownall #1 - 43

Mrs. Pownall: No, right in Charleston, South Carolina.

Admiral Pownall: But I'll tell you this--some of us helped Sims there in Washington. They were glad to get me out of Washington.

Q: You say you helped Admiral Sims in Washington. I think that might be an interesting period in history. What do you mean?

Admiral Pownall: We said, "Why are you doing this? You're just getting yourself in trouble with the Democratic government [who were in office at that time]."

He said, "The day will come when you young fellows will thank me. When I'm pushing up daisies, you'll thank me for going to bat on this." And we have.

Q: This was in connection with keeping the ships in good condition, even though we weren't fighting a war.

Admiral Pownall: That's right.

They had hearings before the Senate Armed Forces Committee. Sims wasn't reprimanded, but we were not popular with the Democrats in office at that time.* I ended up on a destroyer on the way to the Asiatic Station.
_____
*On 9 March 1920, a Senate subcommittee began hearings on the conduct of World War I.

Q: Was that one reason you think you had that duty, because you had helped him out, had supported him?

Admiral Pownall: No.

Mrs. Pownall: No, it was wonderful his getting this brand-new ship and being sent out to the Orient. He went all the way around through the Suez Canal and around the world.

Q: I really want you to tell me. Where did you take command of the USS John D. Ford?

Admiral Pownall: Charleston, South Carolina, nice place.

We sailed with the 43rd Division for Gibraltar on our way to Chefoo, China, with the 43rd and 45th, the two divisions. The 38th was out there.

She went the other way.*

Jock Abbott was our division commander.** We went from Newport to Gib, Gib to Algiers, Algiers to Malta, Malta to Colombo in Ceylon, where I bought my sweetie some nice jewels.

From Colombo we went to Manila. My exec was then a

---
*This is a reference to Mrs. Pownall.
**Commander John S. Abbott, USN.

lieutenant, Jerry Wright.* His father, Bill Wright, was commanding general of the Philippines. My admiral ordered the John D. Ford to go to Manila so that Jerry could see his father. His father had been ordered home sick.

So we left the outfit at Singapore and went up to Manila. We went in there in the dead of night and anchored in all these fishnets, and Jerry got ashore to see his dad. Then I left my exec behind and had to go direct to Chefoo alone.

The boy that took over navigation couldn't navigate very well. He said, "Sir, I don't know where we are, and I don't know how to find out where we are." We were off the Shantung Peninsula. That was a troublesome day. We finally got in. We went through a typhoon on the way; that was some trip.

Mrs. Pownall: They were out of all communications. All of these officers' wives that were with me had received mail, and I hadn't. They didn't know what in the world was the matter. Their husbands had written them and told them not to say anything to me, but they didn't know but what the John D. Ford was lost. They were in this terrible typhoon; they had no radio.

Admiral Pownall: Chefoo, China, is the same place.
―――――――――
*Lieutenant Jerauld Wright, USN, later a four-star admiral.

I had one experience there. My classmate, Holloway Frost, was a War College man.* He had written this thing in our operations, that a destroyer had to get in to 500 yards before he could sink a big ship.

On our cruising around there we had gone to Java. On the way back from Java, the John D. Ford had a pretty close shave. We were chasing the Huron; it was on a dark night, and I had to get in to 500 yards. I was in there on her quarter; she went hard left. There we were--what I did was porpoise across her bow. I succeeded to saving the ship, and I got a "well done." Also, the next thing I knew, I was over on the staff in Holloway's job, and Holloway had my job.

Mrs. Pownall: There was a long period in between.

Admiral Pownall: I know.

The reason I want to get ahead is because to me one of the most interesting periods in my life was the Japanese earthquake, and I was on the staff then as operations officer.**

This time I was sent over on the Huron, and the

---
*Lieutenant Commander Holloway H. Frost, USN.
**About noon on 1 September 1923, Tokyo, Yokohama, Nagoya, and many pleasure resorts were almost totally destroyed by a combination of earthquake, fire, and seawaves. The affected area was about 140 miles in an east-west direction and 110 north-south. Nearly 200,000 people were killed.

Japanese earthquake occurred. We were in Chefoo, then went over to Port Arthur. I think this is history. We were to be entertained by the Japanese president of the South Manchurian Railroad. Mary was in Chefoo. We gave our gals money and went to Port Arthur to be entertained with the Japs. I was an aide and down the middle of the table. My admiral, Admiral Anderson, was up next to the Japs.*

He sent for me and said, "Something's happened in Yokohama, and the Japanese cannot communicate with Yokohama. I want you to go back to the ship and get a destroyer under way with a doctor. Get a good one with a good captain."

Of course, they were all good captains, but this was an especially good one, McCrary by name. He made for Yokohama full speed and went through the Shimonoseki Straits and the Inland Sea--and beat the British down there, incidentally--and wired back what had happened. He had the doctor with him that could do things. It took a lot of doctors for all the trouble. I think that's interesting to me.

Then with the Huron we went over and killed cattle on the hoof--Ike Giffen--and filled up the cold storage with food and medicines and sailed for Yokohama and went in there.** They had another one while we were there. It was a small one; we ran up on anchor chains. Then we went

---
*Admiral Edwin A. Anderson, USN, Commander in Chief Asiatic Fleet, 1922-1923.
**Lieutenant Commander Robert C. Giffen, USN, was executive officer of the USS Huron, the Asiatic Fleet flagship.

to work. We commandeered any ship that had the American flag on it, so we had quite a number. The President said we could expend up in the millions. He raised it from one million to ten million.

We did a lot of things, although the Japs couldn't trust us, I don't think. They had a division of cruisers outside when we were in there, and here we were just there to help.

There was one old Japanese admiral who was pretty good, Kobayashi.* I said, "Sir, we have all this mail coming in to Yokohama. It's your mail; it's not ours. Our destroyers have their decks loaded with it. Where will I put it?"

The Ise was a brand-new battle cruiser. He said, "Shades of Mikado, have them go alongside the Ise. And what's more, they can come aboard and have some of our ice cream at the soda fountain." He told them to keep out of the turrets and the communication rooms. "But other than that, your men are welcome aboard the Ise."

Q: That's probably the only time in history that they had welcomed them aboard.

Mrs. Pownall: They were still just as suspicious as could

---

*It is likely that this refers to Rear Admiral Seizo Kobayashi, Imperial Japanese Navy.

Pownall #1 - 49

be.

Q: This is what year? This is when you were on the staff?

Admiral Pownall: The third of September 1923. Yes.

Q: I want to be sure that we have followed the chronology. You were on the Ford for two years?

Admiral Pownall: Yes.

Q: That would have been, I think, fairly accurate, because you went aboard her in '21.

Mrs. Pownall: You weren't on the Ford two years. You were on the Ford in the United States for about six months, and then you went out there. And it was in the spring after we got out there, which was the spring of '23, that you were transferred.

Q: The biography that you sent me shows that you went to the Navy Department for two years, 1919 and '20. And then in '21 went on the Ford. Then two years later went on the staff of the Huron.

Admiral Pownall: I remember on the earthquake, it was a

terrible thing.

Q: I can't visualize it.

Admiral Pownall: No, you can't.

Mrs. Pownall: I bought some beautiful kimonos over there. When Charles saw them, he said, "I just can't look at those things." When they went up into the harbor, they plowed through these women and children with these beautiful kimonos on. They were all floating around in the water, all dead.

Admiral Pownall: We went up to report to the ambassador. The admiral let me get up in the bow with the coxswain. We tried to dodge these, and finally we got through.

Q: Plowed through the bodies of the dead floating in the harbor?

Admiral Pownall: Yes, all the way up.
 There was one interesting thing--old Cal Barnes, my old skipper, was there. He had a destroyer. We had to get the people out of Tokyo and get them aboard ship, Americans and British. Mrs. J. O. Richardson was one of them.

Q: The wife of Admiral Richardson?*

Admiral Pownall: Yes, May Richardson.

This Jap pilot received instructions not to let American ships, not to let any ship, go up to Tokyo. Here was Cal; he came over on Cal's ship. Cal was getting the anchor up, and he was saying, "You can't go to Tokyo."

Cal said, "You know, when you get an order from your admiral, you just have to go up anchor."

He said, "You can't go up that way.

"When you get an order from your admiral, you have to go full speed ahead both engines."

They were so afraid. They had a division of cruisers watching us. Then, when Oscar Badger brought a load of trucks in, they questioned him very much.** And Oscar said, "I don't want to do anything. I just want to find out where you want these trucks." But they certainly were afraid.

We did so much, and the doctors. We did one thing--the ship--the Barber Line--the captain. We went over to see what she had that we could use, supplies that were needed.

One thing was that the mother of the ambassador didn't have any bed to sleep in. The embassy had been pretty well hit. I was telling this old skipper, "I wish I could get a bed here for the ambassador." I noticed in his cabin was a

---
*Commander James O. Richardson, USN, commanding officer, USS Asheville (PG-21), and Commander South China Patrol.
**Lieutenant Commander Oscar C. Badger, USN, who was on the staff of Commander in Chief Asiatic Fleet.

nice bed, but I wasn't thinking of that. It reminded me that I wanted to get a bed, but I didn't want his bed. The next day over on the Huron came a bed. He had given his own bed.

One other interesting thing--the British were in there also. (I'm British, you know.) I was out on the deck with Admiral Anderson, and a boat came alongside. Admiral Anderson said, "There's a woman in that boat, Pownall. Go down and help her out." And I did. She was the wife of a British merchant or something. She was down at Kamakura, and he had taken her aboard the HMS [I can't think of the name]. They said, "I'm sorry, we can't take women aboard."

She said, "I see an American ship over there. Will you please transfer me to that ship?" Of course, the British changed their tune after that. Of course, it is very seldom that you take womenfolk aboard ship.

Q: Regardless of the emergency.

Admiral Pownall: Yes. So we turned her over to the chaplain.

Mrs. Pownall: You took her aboard.

Admiral Pownall: Yes, we gave her the chaplain's room, put a little toilet in there for her, and she was very happy.

Q: I'm sure it must have been an unbelievable experience for anyone who wasn't there. I'm sure that we did lots for them, but that doesn't last very long. It's like the story, "What did you do for me lately?"

Admiral Pownall: It's hard for me to think that the same people that we were serving in '23 would knife us in the back in Pearl Harbor.

Q: And those days have passed, too, and here we are again in 1970. So times change.

I think those stories are awfully interesting. Do you have anything related to the fact that you were operations officer and fleet athletics officer, as well as aide, at that time?

Admiral Pownall: The around-the-world flight was on, the Army Air Force.

Admiral Washington had relieved Admiral Anderson then.* He went to the river, the Yangtze. Admiral Washington took his chief of staff and one other officer, senior to me, with him. They went up and went around a curve in the Yangtze River, and I couldn't communicate with them. Communications had a funny way that way with waves.

I had to get something in the Whangpoo River to look

---
*Admiral Thomas Washington, USN, Commander in Chief Asiatic Fleet, 1923-25.

out for these pilots when they came through. So I ordered Charles B. McVay--who had the Yangtze patrol; he was a very exacting officer--to put a tug in the Yangtze River.* Admiral Washington was having lunch with him. I'd used the zero-zero on the messages.** I said, "I have to act as if I am an admiral, whether I am or not," so I used zero-zero. Here McVay was having lunch with Admiral Washington in Hankow.

He said, "Here, Admiral, there's somebody on your staff using your zero-zero."

He said, "Yes, he's using my zero-zero. You'd better carry out his orders.

Yes, those were exacting days.

Q: Do you have any more anecdotes that you can recall from your time on the Asiatic Station, Admiral?

Admiral Pownall: Yes. In Shanghai I was taken sick, and I was taken over to the Shanghai General Hospital, expecting to be opened up. The Sisters of Mercy, Belgian, gave me some pills and I didn't have to go. I was carried out of the Palace Hotel on a litter. I came back to the hotel, after I didn't have any operation and after I was well, and

---

*Rear Admiral Charles B. McVay, Jr., USN, Commander Yangtze Patrol.
**The various officers on the staff had code numbers corresponding to their billets. Admiral Washington's number was 00.

saw my daughter with some children playing doctor.

Mrs. Pownall: Carrying this boy down on an ironing board.

Admiral Pownall: To come back to the Palace Hotel and see yourself imitated, being carried out.

Mrs. Pownall: We picked up a wonderful amah there, in Shanghai. We took her down to Manila with us. To make a long story short--she was the number one wife of General Wood's number one boy, the Governor General of the Philippines.*

She stayed with us the whole time, she traveled all over the Orient with us. She was wonderful. Louisa tried to contact her when she went back, when she was grown up, but she couldn't.** That was after the Chinese-Japanese war. We never heard anything more from her.

She said, when we left out there, "I see you sometime, Missy, I see you stateside." When we went up to Bremerton, when Charles was on the Saratoga, I had a telephone call.*** This woman who lived up there said, "Mrs. Pownall, you don't know me, but I have your Chinese amah with me at the ammunition depot. Every ship that has come

---
*General Leonard Wood, USA (Ret.), who had been U. S. Army Chief of Staff, 1910-14, was Governor General of the Philippines, 1921-27.
**Louisa is the Pownalls' daughter.
***Pownall served in the USS Saratoga (CV-3) in 1927-28.

in here, she has said, "Is Master Charlie Pownall on that ship?" So when the <u>Saratoga</u> came in, they found out he was on it, and she telephoned us. She spent every weekend that we were there with us. She had to go back in six months, because they brought her home. They had to take out a bond, just like we did, when they took her out of China. She was simply wonderful. Of course, she had to go back in six months. This woman had a baby, and so she came back with her to take care of it.

Admiral Pownall: Louisa was taken sick. We were up in Baguio. Baguio is a mountain resort back of Manila. Our daughter got sick and had the measles. She rode in an army ambulance, pulled by mules, to take her to the hospital.

We sent down to Manila for her amah. Her amah came up with a canary bird, "Pearly tail" by name. Here was a big old truck coming in with the amah on the front seat with the driver, carrying the canary bird.

Mrs. Pownall: She stayed in the hospital with Louisa all the time she was there.

Q: Measles are kind of newsworthy today, I guess, aren't they?

Mrs. Pownall: I should say they are. She pretty nearly had pneumonia.

Admiral Pownall: They moved an old colonel that had DTs out of the only room that had a bath, and let my daughter have it.* I thought that was a very kind gesture from one service to another. That's an army hospital.

Q: Then you went from Chefoo down to Manila?

Mrs. Pownall: We went up and down with the fleet two years in succession.

Admiral Pownall: We operated in the summer in China and in the winter in Manila, in the Asiatic Fleet.

Q: Do you remember--I'm asking this because Admiral Sabin said I should remind you of a picture that he has taken with you and the Battenberg Cup.**

Do you want to tell me the story about that?

Admiral Pownall: That wasn't the Asiatic Station though.

---
*DTs--delirium tremens, a symptom of intoxication.
**Commander Kitchen had previously interviewed Vice Admiral Lorenzo S. Sabin, USN (Ret.), for the Naval Institute's oral history program. The Battenberg Cup was presented in the years before World War II to the U. S. Navy ship with the fastest pulling whaleboat crew--that is, a whaleboat powered by sailors pulling oars.

Q: I thought it related to this because you were athletic officer at this time.

Admiral Pownall: No, this is the Enterprise, when I was captain of the Enterprise.*

Q: Then we'll wait for that.

I don't like to leave the Asiatic Station if there's more stories to tell.

Mrs. Pownall: We went to Peking twice while we were out there that time. We had a perfectly wonderful Chinese rickshaw boy. He was about six feet, six. I'd never seen anything so big. He could pull a rickshaw with either my daughter and myself, or the amah and my daughter, imagine. That's what he did at the place where we were staying at a hotel in Peking. He was just down below; we could open the window and call him, and he'd be at the front door when we got out there.

Tell about the rice--about the money. Charles always worries about people not getting enough to eat. So before he left, I stayed on.

Admiral Pownall: I asked him whether he had enough. He

---
*Pownall commanded the USS Enterprise (CV-6) from December 1938 to March 1941.

said, "Yes." He wouldn't take any more. He said, "There's a lot of good in those Chinese. I wish they could settle those troubles."

Mrs. Pownall: They were wonderful, that Chinese amah and Chinese boy.

Q: Did it bother you to have someone, human labor, pulling you?

Admiral Pownall: No, he was great big and strong and seemed to enjoy it. I thought that that was overdone--the fact that the new China doesn't have any rickshaws, saying they're bad for the health.

Mrs. Pownall: Jerry, they died very young, even the big ones. We had so many interesting things that happened in China, but I don't know that they have anything at all to do with this.

Admiral Pownall: We went through the forbidden city and saw the Daibutsu, the Quan Yen.

Mrs. Pownall: It was the Emperor's private shrine that he would pray before each day. He was the president then. It had been the Emperor's. It's one solid piece of white jade carved into this Quan Yen. We were allowed to see it, because we were on the admiral's staff. We'd have never gotten in there otherwise.

I'll tell you another thing we saw there, or you can tell this one, about going out and seeing all those courts as we went out. It's sad.

Admiral Pownall: In the courts, they execute for theft. Also, in my destroyer days, we lost a couple of blankets out of a porthole. I was called in to testify against these Chinamen. I said, "What's the penalty?"

They said, "Death."

I said, "Forget it. If they return the blankets, we'll call it square." They had taken a couple of blankets out of the porthole, and of course they were keen to get anything they could.

On my old ship we used to feed a whole family on two of the junks from what we'd throw overboard. And we used them to clean bilges; they were men. One time I remember-- they're crazy for soap. I went back and they were demonstrating with the females, too, in the after washroom, watching the gals take a bath. So we had to close that out. I don't think that's very interesting.

Q: The desire for soap is interesting, I think.

Admiral Pownall: They were pretty nice people in a way. They have no regard for death; it doesn't mean anything to them.

Mrs. Pownall: We were going out to the Temple of Heaven, and as we went out, these carts passed us. Every one of these carts had a coolie standing in it. They were all being taken out to be beheaded, because they had just stolen something. Isn't that awful?

Admiral Pownall: Another thing we can tell about Chefoo-- we were in a missionary home. I was going on the staff, right from the Ford, and they were giving a farewell party. Our amah was looking out for Louisa; she was little. The mistress of this missionary home struck our amah. And I said, "That's terrible."

Mrs. Pownall: Everything was supposed to be closed up there right after dinner, and we hadn't gotten home. So she stayed with Louisa, and when she went back to her room this woman who was running this home wouldn't believe that she had been with her and hadn't been off someplace else. So she struck her, she beat her. That's how little they think about--and that woman was English.

Admiral Pownall: Then we moved to the Astor House, before

we went over to Port Arthur. At the Astor House, we had a room over the barroom, until we could get something else because the place was jammed.

We were over the barroom, and I remember Louisa, about so big, said, "Daddy, what is a son of a bitch?" It was that sort of life inside there.

Mrs. Pownall: These bluejackets would come in there, you know, and she'd hear them.

Q: Do we want to depart from the Asiatic Fleet and come back to the Navy Department?

Admiral Pownall: I came back to the Navy Department, and went to the Bureau of Engineering.

Q: I think it's interesting, as Mrs. Pownall said, every tour you had of shore duty was in Washington.

Mrs. Pownall: They'd ask for him back. Every time he asked to go to the Naval War College, but there was always somebody in Washington who wanted him right back there. So he never got to the Naval War College. He got selected anyway.*

Admiral Pownall: Then, when I was in the Bureau of Engineering, Admiral Ghormley asked me to have lunch with the Assistant Secretary.** Right after that, I was transferred. I didn't stay in the Bureau of Engineering very long, I went as his aide, aide to the Assistant Secretary of the Navy. He, Mr. Robinson, was very pro-aviation.

We had arrived in a Faulkner plane, with Mrs. Pownall there. They stopped the engines and started them and gave us a real thrill. I put in for aviation and was accepted.

I went down to Pensacola. There is my class at Pensacola. That's a year's production. [Apparently looking at a picture.] Alongside of me is Harry Bogusch-- he's one of the old guys.*** Alongside of Harry, in the first row is Johnny Waldron, who was killed at Midway.**** That's all we could produce in two years.

Q: How many are in that class, about 25?

---
*This refers to Pownall's eventual selection for promotion to flag rank. Many of the Pownall's contemporaries who became admirals did have the benefit of attendance at the Naval War College.
**Commander Robert L. Ghormley, USN, later a flag officer in World War II, served in 1923-24 as aide to Assistant Secretary of the Navy Theodore Roosevelt, Jr., and in 1924-25 as aide to Assistant Secretary T. Douglas Robinson. Pownall relieved Ghormley.
***Lieutenant Commander Harry R. Bogusch, USN.
****Lieutenant (junior grade) John C. Waldron, USN, who was killed on 4 June 1942 while in command of Torpedo Squadron Eight.

Admiral Pownall: About that. That was it, one enlisted man.

Q: You became a naval aviator in March 1927?*

Admiral Pownall: I got my wings before that. I got my wings and then was kept over to take the advanced course. So I had my wings long before that.

Q: Tell me something about your experiences at Pensacola, what the training duty was like.

Admiral Pownall: It was exacting.

One of our old colored gals said, "Don't you fly that airplane, Lieutenant. You let Jesus do it."

In gunnery, I had a forced landing, which was something. In gunnery you're supposed to hit the sleeve of a towing plane. The plane tows the sleeve, and you're supposed to put the bullets in the sleeve. I was so intense on this, I hit the airplane with the sleeve. Of course, the airplane stopped.

Here I was up over the Gulf at Pensacola in a fog--it was foggy, too--with the sleeve wrapped around my prop. Fortunately, the cloud opened up a little bit, and I sideslipped through and landed on the beach. That was my first real forced landing.

---

*Admiral Pownall's official Navy biography indicates that he was designated a naval aviator on 30 March 1927.

I had another one, but out in the bay. Somebody saw my bald head and came back and said, "Baldy Pownall has had a forced landing." So they automatically came out and got me.

I was a good training. I enjoyed it. It happened that Harry Bogusch and I--eight old fellows started, and only two of us got through.*

Q: Who were the others that started with you? You were older than . . .

Admiral Pownall: . . . than the regular class. Bogusch was a class below me at the Naval Academy. I can't remember the others.

Admiral King came down later.** He was a plebe when I was a first classman at Pensacola. We were friends and he asked me--should he take this stunt course. He was a man in his years; he was a captain. He had to leave soon to go to his daughter's wedding.*** I told him to obey his instructor. If his instructor said he was a good pilot, forget age and go out and do it. And he did. That night he left, right after passing the stunt check. We had a nice party before he went back to Annapolis to his

---
*Bogusch had been graduated from the Naval Academy in 1911, a year after Pownall.
**Captain Ernest J. King, USN, was designated a naval aviator on 26 May 1927. King was later Chief of Naval Operations during World War II.
***Elizabeth King, married in that spring of 1927, was the first of King's five daughters to become a bride.

daughter's wedding.

Mary, on Friday nights, used to make the best mint juleps. The more mint juleps she gave us, the better we flew.

Mrs. Pownall: The whole class used to come to our house. They never were allowed to take a drink except on Friday and Saturday. They had to sober up on Sunday, and go back on Monday. They weren't allowed to drink during the week at all. So they certainly had parties on the weekends. They didn't get tight at our house. They'd come there right after they left the school. Then I'd make mint juleps for them, because it was as hot as could be. Then they'd go someplace else and go on some kind of a party.

Q: Were you the only married officer there?

Admiral Pownall: No, Bogusch was married.

Mrs. Pownall: Admiral King's family weren't there.

Admiral Pownall: From Pensacola, I was ordered as navigator of the USS Saratoga. That was a very happy ship.

Q: You went aboard her when she was fitting out?

Admiral Pownall: At the New York Shipbuilding Company.*

    Admiral Mitscher was the air officer, Jimmy Alexander was the engineer officer, and I was the navigator.** The first thing to do was to get that old ship--she was big, she scared us. She was the biggest thing in the Navy then.

Q: Nobody had seen anything bigger than that, at that point, had they?

Admiral Pownall: That's right.

    One thing--we had to move her over to the Philadelphia Navy Yard. There were a lot of tides and currents in the Delaware River. My chief quartermaster and myself were not satisfied with the tide tables and the current tables. So we started some research of our own, with a buoy in the river, when the flood tide was slack, and so on. We found that the current and tide tables were out quite a bit. So when it came time to move her, when the river pilots came down to move her, I said, "It isn't time yet, sir."

    Captain Yarnell said, "The pilots think it's time to go now.***

---

*The shipyard was at Camden, New Jersey.
**Lieutenant Commander Marc A. Mitscher, USN, later a carrier task force commander in World War II; Lieutenant Commander James T. Alexander, USN.
***Captain Harry E. Yarnell, USN, later a four-star admiral, was the first commanding officer of the USS Saratoga (CV-3).

I said, "Not according to my book."

He said, "I think they know more than you do."

"All right, sir."

So we pushed the old *Saratoga* out, flood tide caught her, and if we'd hit the buoy up the river, we'd have been aground.

Yarnell, God bless him, came to me and said, "May I see that little book? And how many more minutes is it to slack water?" Fortunately, it was not too many that we didn't hit the buoy, but he had a lot of respect for my little book after that. So did the river pilots, too.

We got her in and fitted her out. Then, when we went down the river, she was big. We met a merchant ship coming up, a tanker. There was a very narrow place at Chester, on the Delaware River. We knew if we touched the buoy, we'd touch the rock. I was on the starboard side, and I had to say how many feet to the buoy. The last one I reported was a foot and a half; that's how close we came. We just slid through. This little Dutchman wouldn't give an inch.

Q: You were the biggest ship afloat at that point, weren't you?

Admiral Pownall: We had sent out notices, but it didn't make any difference to this Dutchman. He came up the river anyway.

Mrs. Pownall: They had sent out word that nothing was to come up the river at the time that big thing went down.

Admiral Pownall: Of course, the city of Philadelphia controlled the river as far as Chester. But beyond that, it was anybody's river, so to speak. All the city of Philadelphia had was the old Matt Quay, which was nothing but a tug. This fellow went right by him as if he hadn't been there. But we got her out. She was a very happy ship, and I learned a lot. Ken Whiting was exec.*

Q: Ken Whiting is quite a historical and dramatic character, isn't he?

Admiral Pownall: Oh, yes.

Mrs. Pownall: He had himself shot out of a torpedo tube and came back in again. Did you know that? He had been on submarines. He wanted to see whether it could be done, and he did it. He really was a wonderful person. They were very close friends. I stayed with them out in Honolulu.

Q: He's almost legendary. You don't really believe that he lives, because he did so many things.

---
*Commander Kenneth Whiting, USN.

Admiral Pownall: Pete was our air officer, and a good one. Jimmy Alexander was the engineer officer. There were three classmates--Mitscher, Alexander, and Pownall. Alexander was the senior.

Mrs. Pownall: He got out of the Navy before selection for admiral.

Q: It must have been an exciting experience being on the Saratoga.

Admiral Pownall: Oh, yes. She was big.

Q: Can you tell me where she went and what she did? You were there for about a year and some months. I was just thinking of some chronology of what your experiences aboard the Saratoga were during her operations.

Admiral Pownall: We had flight operations, we had four squadrons, and we were in war problems.

Q: Didn't you come through the canal to the West Coast?

Admiral Pownall: Yes, we did.

Pownall #1 - 71

Mrs. Pownall: That was another thing that Charles had to be very careful about. He went through first, and he got through all right. But when the Lexington went through, which was exactly the same size, they took the lamp posts off the canal.* But Charles had had it all worked out, and he got through all right.

Q: This was at the time you were aboard her the first time?

Admiral Pownall: Yes.

Q: She was stationed in Long Beach?

Admiral Pownall: Yes.

Q: Who was the skipper of the Saratoga then?

Admiral Pownall: Captain Harry Yarnell.

Before that, it had been Captain Butler.** Captain Butler is about six feet, three, and I'm about five feet, six. Our bridge I couldn't see over from my five feet,

---
*Vice Admiral A. M. Pride's Naval Institute oral history discusses this incident. Pride was in the Lexington (CV-2) when she went through the Panama Canal the first time.
**Captain Henry V. Butler, USN, was designated as prospective commanding officer of the Saratoga, but Captain Yarnell took over from him prior to the ship's commissioning on 16 November 1927.

six. I didn't get much sympathy from Butler, because he was a big, tall man.

Then Harry Yarnell came, and he was just about an inch taller than I was. So we had to take the navy yard crowd to sea to lower the bridge rail so we could see over it.

I was there a year in fleet operations. Then I went over to the Lexington as air officer. John Halligan came to relieve Yarnell.*

I'll also tell about the fog, with Harry Yarnell--we came into Bremerton and just did get in. It was very foggy. We anchored at Admiralty Inlet. The Saratoga was due at the navy yard the next morning. Captain Yarnell said, "Pownall, suppose we go up, fog or no fog."

I said, "All right." I had one of the Fathometers, a new thing, that measures the depth of the floor of the channel or ocean. When you navigate with it, you know what depth the water is and whether you're safe.

Old Ken Whiting came up to look things over in the charthouse, and he said, "How does this damn thing work?" And he whacked it and put it out of business. I didn't want to say anything. I never said anything about it. But we went up anyway, in the fog. The only thing, we were afraid we might meet another ship. The Saratoga was on the side nearest the shore. But we got in all right.

---
*Captain John Halligan, Jr., USN.

Pownall #1 - 73

Q: What were you taking her to Bremerton for?

Admiral Pownall: For overhaul, a lot of work. When a ship is new that way and you're out of the shipbuilder's yard, there's a lot of work that the Navy had to do itself, particularly in gunnery. And that's why we went there.

Mrs. Pownall: You had been through an awful lot of maneuvers. You were with the fleet down in southern waters before you came up there.

Admiral Pownall: Then I went to the Lexington.

Mrs. Pownall: Admiral Yarnell was relieved right after that. He put his arm around Charles and said, "Pownall, no matter what, don't let anybody tell you to go into a fog like that, like I did."

Admiral Pownall: I went over to the Lexington, which was an entirely different ship. They had a different organization. They had what's called the X and Y system. On the Saratoga, it was just straight chain of command. Squadrons reported to the air officer, and the air officer reported to the exec, and the exec reported to the captain. On the Lexington, they had this funny thing, they had X and Y departments. The people that flew could sidetrack the air officer, and when they did they'd generally get into trouble, because it didn't work out very well.

I said, when I was ordered over--I went to the admiral, "I would rather not go as air officer, unless we take the Saratoga's system." That was Admiral Reeves.* He waited a day. He had to think it over.

Then he said, "We'll change the Lexington's to the Saratoga's system." And we did. It made a big difference, believe me.

Before I'd gone as air officer, two good men had come to trouble--Bobby Molten and Squash Griffen.**

Q: Tell me what you mean, they had gotten into trouble.

Admiral Pownall: Conflict of orders--people were issuing them orders direct, instead of through the air officer.

So the X and Y system went out of the Navy forever. Reeves was the admiral. Frank Berrien was the captain of the ship.*** I remember Berrien very well; he was an old destroyer man. He was out flying one day and he came back, in a torpedo plane, and I was on the bridge. He got out of that plane and walked right through a propeller. It wasn't in sequence to hit him.

---
*Rear Admiral Joseph M. Reeves, USN, was then Commander Aircraft Squadrons Battle Fleet.
**Lieutenant Commander Robert P. Molten, Jr., USN; Lieutenant Commander Virgil C. Griffin, Jr., USN.
***Captain Frank D. Berrien, USN, commanding officer of the Lexington.

Q: You mean it didn't kill him?

Admiral Pownall: No, it didn't touch him. The old torpedo plane propeller, four blades. Just turning over slowly, and he just walked through the propeller.

Q: I bet he was scared afterwards though, when he realized what he had done.

Admiral Pownall: We gave him the devil.

Mrs. Pownall: I think the thing was he didn't see it.

Q: Probably not, I wouldn't think he'd do it on purpose.

Admiral Pownall: He didn't do it deliberately. When you got out of a torpedo plane, you're supposed to watch what you're doing. He just got down off the wing and walked through.

The _Lexington_ was a good ship.

Q: Was the _Lexington_ operating on the West Coast? Were you still on the West Coast, operating with the fleet?

Admiral Pownall: Yes. Then from the Lexington, I was aviation officer on the Commander Battle Force staff under Admiral Nulton.*

Q: What was the flagship?

Admiral Pownall: The California.

One thing I can say, that Nulton was a very fine man, but he hated an airplane, and anything connected with an airplane he did not like. Another thing was a Marine--he didn't like Marines or airplanes or aviators. So we might have an argument or two.

E. O. Ames was the Marine, and I was the aviator.** We'd be invited to our respective rooms, because of something that took place. So I'd offer the ladder to E. O., and E. O. would offer it to me.

I thought, "Boy, I'm getting awful marks on this ship." When I looked at my fitness report, I had a 4.0 from Louie Nulton.

Q: Did you have problems with the conflict between what they used to say was "the blackshoe Navy" and aviators?***

---
*Admiral Louis M. Nulton, USN, Commander in Chief Battle Fleet.
**Captain Evans O. Ames, USMC.
***"Blackshoe" is a term applied to battleship-cruiser-destroyer officers to distinguish them from "brownshoe" aviators.

Admiral Pownall: The trouble with Louie was he was afraid something would happen to the planes.

I'd say, "Sir, we ought to launch planes today."

He'd say, "Don't you think it's a little rough?"

"Oh," I'd say, "somebody might bust a strut."

He'd say, "That's just it."

He didn't want to bust a strut. Of course, you'd bust struts all the time with airplanes. But he was very careful and very considerate. I think he made a good Superintendent of the Naval Academy. And he was a perfect gentleman.

Mrs. Pownall: Charles relieved Gene Wilson.* Gene Wilson later became president of United Aircraft.

Admiral Pownall: I relieved him. He retired and went in the industry. He was class of 1908, two years ahead of me.

Mrs. Pownall: Then we went east together to Washington.

Admiral Pownall: Then I went to flight division of the Bureau of Aeronautics.

Q: I have something in between there--from May until

---
*Commander Eugene E. Wilson, USN.

August you were on the Saratoga before you came back to Washington.

Mrs. Pownall: Yes. He came back on the Saratoga with the admiral who was on the Saratoga. He had gone east on the battleship, and they let him come back. He took somebody else's place temporarily. Then he was to go back with us; his tour of duty wasn't quite up. You came through the canal and came back.

Admiral Pownall: Admiral Horne.*

Q: You were Commander Aircraft Squadrons in the Battle Fleet on the Saratoga from May until August?

Admiral Pownall: Yes, a very short time.

Then I went to BuAer and had flight division. I had the engineering section the time before, power plant experimental.**

This time I went as the head of the flight division and started the cadet program. We took kids first, hoping to make pilots of them, out of colleges. The first requirement was that he be a college graduate. Next we

---
*Captain Frederick J. Horne, USN, Commander Aircraft Squadrons, Battle Fleet.
**Pownall headed the power plant and experimental section of the Bureau of Aeronautics from 1930 to 1933 and the flight division from 1936 to 1938.

reduced it to two years. Still we couldn't get enough, so we had to start a school of our own, preflight school. We put them in various universities. We had one in Iowa State. Then one at St. Mary's was a big one. We took the whole college over there.

Q: Weren't you working on some new type of engine there in BuAer?

Admiral Pownall: I was in the Bureau of Aeronautics and had the engineering experimental division in '30.

Q: My notes say that you were head of the power plant and experimental section during the early development of the two-row radial engine.

Admiral Pownall: Just before the jets.

Q: Tell me what that means.

Admiral Pownall: Two-row radial--one row of cylinders--and then right up against it--see you can't build an engine with nothing but a barn door ahead of you. You wouldn't get anywhere. So we had to put the two rows of cylinders bang up against each other, and be sure and ventilate them

Pownall #1 - 80

so they wouldn't burn up. And that was a two-row radial. It was a radial engine that had two rows, one alongside of the other.

Q: What did that accomplish as compared to what had happened before?

Admiral Pownall: About 200 horsepower more. Airlines used them and we used them. The end of the two-row radial was the jet.

When we studied jets at Columbia, they were turned down, because they used so much fuel and they were considered to some extent dangerous. So the jet was held off a year, and this two-row radial took its place.

Both Curtiss Wright and Pratt & Whitney had a two-row Wasp. Then we got Curtiss Wright to make a two-row radial also, so they could be competitors.

We had the air-cooled development. And the Army had the liquid-cooled engine, too. I guess the air-cooled seemed to be better than the liquid-cooled; it won out.

Q: Did you actually help in the invention of it?

Admiral Pownall: Yes, I did to this extent--I worked with the people at Pratt & Whitney. Jimmy Alexander said I had something to do with it. But I didn't work over a drafting board that way exactly. We gave them a contract to make a two-row radial engine according to certain specifications.

Q: And you would prepare the specifications?

Admiral Pownall: That's right.

Mrs. Pownall: And also recommended it highly.

Q: Someone had to back it before they would go ahead and build it, because no one would buy it.
   Was Moffett involved with that?*

Admiral Pownall: He was the Chief of the Bureau.
   One thing about Moffett--he said, "You report to me on this development business. I'm very much interested in it." So I reported direct to the chief of the bureau. I didn't have to go through the steps on the way up, which made it very nice. I did, out of courtesy, but I didn't have to. Old Billy Moffett was a great man. I can say this--he wanted us not to waste the taxpayers' money. So he said, "When you get your experimental program all fixed up, you go out to Dayton and take it up with the Army Air Corps and see where we duplicate or we don't."
   So I got my business together and flew out and

---
*Rear Admiral William A. Moffett, USN, was Chief of the Bureau of Aeronautics from 1920 to 1933.

landed at Dayton. We taxied up, and the plane alongside of me had painted on the side, "General says jump." It happened that the fellow that had been in there before had a bad landing gear, and General Conger Pratt said to go out and jump.* He said, "That's a nice welcome I gave you, but don't jump."

We went over this experimental program and we were getting to pull together, the Air Corps and ourselves. I went back all full of thinking there wouldn't be any problem with the Air Corps.

Then one of the Air Corps generals spilled the beans at a hearing about money. Moffett said, "All those good understandings are finished now. They want to take over the Navy air, and I won't have it." That was when Mitchell came in.**

Q: That was the beginning of the conflict between the two activities? Was that back during the time when you were with the assistant secretary?

Admiral Pownall: Yes, that's right.

---

*Brigadier General Henry Conger Pratt, USA, Assistant Chief of the Army Air Corps, 1930-34.
**Brigadier General William Mitchell, USA, was an outspoken advocate of military aviation. In 1925 he was court-martialed for insubordination because of his criticism of the War and Navy departments for mismanagement of their aviation programs.

Pownall #1 - 83

Q: Do you want to expand on that? It sounds interesting.

Admiral Pownall: I went on a trip with Mr. Robinson. He wanted to make sure that things were all right at sea, with naval aviators and non-aviators. He'd write letters back to the Secretary of the Navy. I did a lot of writing. But Mitchell didn't take over.

We sank a battleship or two at the proving grounds. Of course, you could do that, just anchor a ship and then sink it with a bomb.

Q: Were you involved with that?

Admiral Pownall: No. I was involved in the engine business and also with the assistant secretary, but I wasn't involved in the actual bombing. That was Bruce Leighton.*

Q: If you had an interesting story to tell I didn't want you to not tell it just because it was out of sequence, I wanted to hear it.

Admiral Pownall: Also, the constant speed propeller was a development at that time. It happened the propeller section was under the power plant section.

―――――――――
*Lieutenant Commander Bruce G. Leighton, USN.

Pownall #1 - 84

Mrs. Pownall: Then he went to the Ranger, as executive officer.

Q: Did you take part in the fitting out of the Ranger as well?

Admiral Pownall: Yes. I was there a whole year at Newport News.

Q: Can you tell me something about the Ranger and its fitting out?

Admiral Pownall: She was a five and ten cent store carrier.

Q: What does that mean?

Admiral Pownall: We ran out of tonnage. The Saratoga and Lexington had taken all the treaty tonnage. There was 15,000 tons left, which is not enough for a good aircraft carrier.

But the Republicans, Hoover, built it anyway.* So we used to call it the Hoover carrier, which was not very

---

*Herbert C. Hoover was President of the United States from 1929 to 1933. His wife was the sponsor of the Ranger (CV-4).

nice for President Hoover, also the five and ten cent store carrier because she was so small.

First, she didn't have any island. We were supposed to do it with a flush deck and everything was below decks, the bridge and everything. I finally convinced the Navy Department that the darn thing wouldn't work. So we built an island on her and rearranged . . .

Q: Do I understand you to say that "I," that "you" convinced them to build the island?

Admiral Pownall: I helped to convince them, because you couldn't control airplanes without an island of some kind.

Then we had to think about the smokestacks. So we had them put the stacks out the side. You've seen pictures of that thing. That was the old Ranger.

Q: Tell me how you went about convincing the Navy Department to put an island on it.

Admiral Pownall: I don't know--we'd draw pictures. The thing was--what to do about the oil to balance her. The naval constructors worked that out. There was a lot of good reasons for it, and we produced those reasons. So we had an island, a small island, but it sure enough was an island with a bridge, and you could see to operate aircraft from it.

Q: What had made them think they were going to make one without an island, lack of money?

Admiral Pownall: Lack of money was one thing. But also there were a lot of old aviators who couldn't see anything but a flush flight deck, nothing to interfere with the planes. That wasn't practical.

The Langley was the first one. She didn't have any island.

This is interesting--they wanted us to fly airplanes in the wintertime. So the Ranger was designated to go to Alaska and operate aircraft in the Arctic. We went up to the Cook Inlet and operated aircraft. We did all right, except we went up until the ice came down and hit us. For one thing, we learned a lot. We learned that if you could get up over the clouds, you were in the nicest sunshine. Nobody got hurt. We carried out our flight instructions.

Bristol was sick one day.* I ran the ship. I ran into--an iceberg came down to meet me, and I thought that was far enough.

Q: Tell me about that, you make it sound so casual.

*Captain Arthur L. Bristol, USN, was the first commanding officer of the Ranger.

Admiral Pownall: We didn't realize that salt water freezes at 27 degrees Fahrenheit. We didn't have it very cold up there. We couldn't operate because of the ice. It wasn't the temperature; it was the ice.

We proved a lot about lubricating oil and gasoline, what to do and what not to do, what to do when things were cold, how to get an engine warmed up. We found out a lot of things about operating aircraft.

We came back here to San Diego. When you came into port the whole thing was, "What ship is that?" We met the Langley out there at the entrance to the harbor. Art Davis, our old air officer on the Ranger, was then back on the Langley.*

We said, "The USS Ranger, 40 days out of Kodiak." Then we asked, "What ship is that?"

"The USS Langley. We've been out all night." Yes, we were real sailors.

One thing interesting--when we went up there Prohibition was in then. There was no liquor allowed aboard. We were going into the Arctic, and there was no liquor aboard, not even in the medical department.

So I told Mary--please if there was a safe way to, get me a half a gallon of whiskey, which she did. Bristol had

---

*Commander Arthur C. Davis, USN, was executive officer of the Langley. In June 1934, as a lieutenant commander, Davis made the first landing aboard the Ranger.

the same idea. And the medical officer of the ship thought we ought to have whiskey. So we had whiskey; it was all under the medical department. We were prepared, although according to the regulations, we weren't supposed to have it.

Kids would get wringing wet in the boat. The doctor would put them to bed and give them eggs and a drink of whiskey. That was the standard procedure, whether they were pilots or enlisted boys or whatever they were. It worked pretty good; we didn't lose anybody.

Q: It must have been a cruel winter.

Admiral Pownall: It was.

Q: We're getting to the <u>Langley</u>, as Commander Aircraft Base Force, chief of staff and aide. Was that Admiral King? I have that June '36 to June '37, as a year.

Admiral Pownall: That's right, I was his chief of staff.*

Q: Tell me about that. Where were you and what did you do?

---

*Rear Admiral Ernest J. King, USN, Commander Aircraft Base Force, 1936-37.

Admiral Pownall: King was as bright as could be. We might have arguments, and then he'd say, "Let's play golf. Let's forget it and play golf this afternoon." The next time I'd have to say that. He wouldn't say it two days running.

Q: Was he a difficult man to work for?

Admiral Pownall: Yes, I'm afraid so. No, I won't say that. We got along.

Q: I'm sure I'm difficult to work for. But I don't think that's any particular criticism. Some people just demand a lot.

Admiral Pownall: No, Admiral King was all right, a little difficult but all right.

Q: I believe that's his reputation. So it isn't saying anything new or revealing any secret.
   Where were you and what did you do?

Admiral Pownall: At Coronado.
   We had a new patrol plane. He was going to take it down to Panama. He was to get aboard at Acapulco. We were on the _Wright_. _Wright_ was his flagship.

He asked me what clothes to take with him. I said, "You'd better take your civilian clothes. They're going to entertain you down there." So he took all his nice summer clothes. He took his watch that his mother had given him.

I personally had a couple of boats, because I wasn't quite sure of this plane, although it had a good pilot. The plane took off at Acapulco and hit a swell and went in, and off went King and all his baggage and everything else. It was all lost.

He said, looking right up and down like hazing a plebe, "Did you tell me to take those summer clothes along? I can't take them now; they're at the bottom of Acapulco."

Mrs. Pownall: The awful part was that you saw his plane turn over, and you didn't know but what he was going to drown. Everybody was standing there, but nobody could do anything about it.

Admiral Pownall: It was an experimental patrol plane, and he was very much interested in it and was taking it down to Panama.*

Q: You were the chief of staff as well as the aide, weren't you?

---

*The aircraft was an XP3D. The incident is described in detail in Lieutenant Commander Gerald T. Morton, USN (Ret.), "Sixty Seconds to Live," U. S. Naval Institute Proceedings, September 1985, pages 70-72.

Pownall #1 - 91

Admiral Pownall: I was chief of staff and aide, yes.

Q: Were you a commander by then?

Admiral Pownall: Yes.

Q: You surely had duty on the old-time carriers, didn't you? So you actually were on all four of them.

Admiral Pownall: Yes.

Q: Then you went back to duty in the bureau again. That was when you were head of flight division.

Admiral Pownall: Yes, and we started the cadet program.

Q: The other one was when you were doing experimental work with the engine.
    You were back in Washington for another tour. Where did you live then?

Admiral Pownall: We lived in Somerset, Dorset Avenue. It's right beyond the line between Maryland and Washington.

Mrs. Pownall: The street that we lived on, just a little bit beyond where we were, was lined with the cherry blossom trees that were given for that part of it.

We lived in an old farmhouse that had been all done over. This Doctor Jaffee bought this and he put up four or five of the loveliest houses, but we had the old farmhouse, which was just lovely. And we had beautiful big trees in the front, and a whole orchard of different kinds of fruit trees in the back. It was just lovely. We only lived there about a year and a half.

The reason we left there was that he went to the <u>Enterprise</u>.

Q: I was wondering why your tour of duty was so short there.

Admiral Pownall: I was in the flight division one day when Newt White came into the office and said, "Charlie, how would you like to take the <u>Enterprise</u>?"*

I said, "Why, sure, I'd like to take the <u>Enterprise</u>."

He said, "This morning we'll see Admiral Joe Richardson." So we went in to see Admiral Joe, he was in the Bureau of Navigation.** To make a long story short, I

---
*Captain Newton H. White, Jr., USN, was commanding officer of the <u>Enterprise</u> (CV-6) when the ship was commissioned on 12 May 1938. Captain Pownall relieved him of command on 21 December 1938.
**Rear Admiral James O. Richardson, USN, was Chief of the Bureau of Navigation, 1938-39.

was slated to command the *Enterprise*, which was, to me, a great thing.

Q: Don't make a long story short. Tell me about the details.

Admiral Pownall: Which to me was a great thing.

Q: Admiral Richardson was then the head of the Bureau of Navigation (which was the same thing as Personnel).

Weren't you fortunate? You have had just exceedingly marvelous duties.

Mrs. Pownall: Every time he came out of Washington, he had a brand-new ship.

Q: So I've observed, yes. At least it's unique with the men with whom I've had association.

Admiral Pownall: She was a wonderful ship, with a wonderful crew, and wonderful officers.

Q: Now you had just made captain, of course, or you wouldn't have been given the job. So you were a fresh captain and fresh head of the *Enterprise*. Weren't you lucky?

Admiral Pownall: Yes, I was.

Q: How come?

Admiral Pownall: I don't know, I didn't have anything to do with it.

Mrs. Pownall: You didn't have any pull, but you had an awful lot of friends.

Q: You must have always done a spectacularly fine job.

Admiral Pownall: I tried to do my best.

Mrs. Pownall: I think it was his friends. These senior officers that he was associated with thought an awful lot of him.

Q: The reason they thought a lot of him was because he had done a fine job.

Admiral Pownall: There were two men that thought well of me, Nimitz and James Forrestal.* C. W. Nimitz was a good

―――――――――
*James V. Forrestal was Secretary of the Navy from 1944 to 1947.

friend.

Another man that I met on the Enterprise was Adolphus Andrews. The Enterprise was his flagship. The Enterprise was flagship to Adolphus Andrews and to Joe Richardson.*

Q: I want you to tell me the details about the Enterprise--where you went, what you were part of, where you operated, and who were the men involved.

Admiral Pownall: I took command of her at Christmas of '38 at Norfolk.

Then, I will say this, Norfolk Navy Yard was having trouble. The first day after I got aboard the Enterprise, the catapult blew up. They found thermite in the case where the catapult was.

Q: That's an explosive substance, isn't it?

Admiral Pownall: An explosive that had been put there purposely, for sabotage. The clues were cold.

The next thing that happened, we found some of the arresting gear was cut through with a hacksaw. Whereupon I

---
*Vice Admiral Adolphus Andrews, USN, Commander Scouting Force. In June 1939, Richardson was promoted to full admiral and made Commander Battle Force.

went to Admiral Smith, who had the district.*

But I had to get the ship out of there, because there was something going on then. The workmen were hard up, and the Enterprise was their breadbasket. The Enterprise would be a breadbasket for the Navy Yard workmen.

Q: Were they trying to delay her?

Admiral Pownall: Yes, trying to delay her. I couldn't prove it, but I know darn well they were.

I said, "I'd like to get over to the operating base. I'll take her over myself."

"No," he said, "you don't have to do that."

So we went over to the operating base. With the ship's force and a few helpers, we finished the ship. Then we went to Guantanamo and joined the fleet. We got out a lot earlier than we would have otherwise.

Q: You did go through the canal, and out to the West Coast?

Admiral Pownall: Yes. Admiral Halsey was the division commander.** He had the Enterprise and Yorktown.

---
*This reference is unclear. Rear Admiral Joseph K. Taussig, USN, was then commandant of the Fifth Naval District, and Rear Admiral Manley H. Simons, USN, was commandant of the Norfolk Navy Yard.
**Rear Admiral William F. Halsey, Jr., USN, Commander Carrier Division Two.

Q: What ships did you travel with?

Mrs. Pownall: It was '39 now, and you were all to go to the exposition. They had trouble and the war had broken out, or they were afraid they were going to have war or something.

They ordered you to go on out, and you thought they were going to send you straight out to Singapore. But you didn't; you went out to the West Coast and stayed there.

Admiral Pownall: We had orders we couldn't open until we got out to a certain longitude.

Adolphus Andrews had that task force, and he used the Enterprise as flagship. Ping Wilkinson, a wonderful fellow, was the chief of staff. He stood first in his class.*

We went to the exposition in San Francisco. I had said, "If the crew want a race boat, the captain does."

Old Kelly, who had been on the California race boats crew, came in and wanted to see the captain. He said, "Sir, I've sounded out the crew, and we want a race boat. And we'll race in San Francisco at the fair."

The next thing I knew, they'd turned in their liberty

---

*Captain Theodore S. Wilkinson, USN, chief of staff to Commander Scouting Force.

cards. They were so anxious to win that race that they gave up their own liberty. I said, "I guess if you win the race, you won't need a liberty card."

They won the race, and each got a $20.00 gold piece from the city of San Francisco. It was a great day.

Q: How long did you stay at the exposition?

Admiral Pownall: Maybe ten days.

Then we went back to Coronado. At the time we went out, all this excitement was going on in the Pacific. We didn't know whether we'd go on to Singapore or not. Too bad we didn't because that was just the time the war broke out and the British lost their two battleships--the Repulse and the Prince of Wales. Had we gone on, if they'd let us go, we probably could have avoided this.*

Q: You could have avoided the British losing their ships? How did you figure you could have done that?

Admiral Pownall: We'd have gone to war right then.

Q: You would have initiated the war, you mean?

---

*Admiral Pownall was evidently confused on this point. The Prince of Wales and Repulse were sunk in December 1941. He had been relieved of command of the Enterprise on 21 March of that year by Captain George D. Murray, USN.

Pownall #1 - 99

Admiral Pownall: We would have protected those ships, that's all.

Q: With your planes?

Admiral Pownall: Yes, we had a nice group of squadrons.

Q: Then did you operate from Coronado? These are getting to be exciting war years. That is, the danger is building up in the Pacific. When did you go out to the Pacific?

Admiral Pownall: Not until spring of '40.

Q: You were on the Enterprise all through '39 and '40, and through March of '41. I was just interested in where the Enterprise was and what her operations were.

This is such an interesting period of history. When Admiral Richardson, as I understand, did not want the fleet out there (at Pearl Harbor) and went back and made his presentation and never returned.*

Admiral Pownall: He had the Enterprise as his flagship. I remember this--that he had us man our antiaircraft

---

*Richardson made this presentation to President Franklin D. Roosevelt in the fall of 1940 while serving as Commander in Chief U. S. Fleet. Richardson was relieved of the fleet command on 1 February 1941 by Admiral Husband E. Kimmel, USN.

batteries early every morning and in the evening.

He wrote an essay when he was at the War College that sooner or later the Japs would strike Pearl Harbor. Of course, he went to the President and told him he didn't like to keep the fleet in Pearl Harbor. The President sort of dressed him down.

Q: Did he return, or was he relieved when he was in Washington?

Admiral Pownall: He wasn't relieved until he got back out there; he turned over to Kimmel.

Mrs. Pownall: I know all that so well, because Mrs. Richardson was staying with me.

Admiral Pownall: On the _Enterprise_ also the Secretary of the Navy came out to size up who would be the next commander in chief. I turned my cabin over to SecNav Knox.*

To me it was terrible, I was so fond of J. O. Richardson. Here they were just ready to crucify him, it seemed to me.

Q: Again, that is a common feeling of people. I know of no one who had anything to do with him that just didn't

---
*Frank Knox was Secretary of the Navy from 1940 to 1944.

give him the highest regards.

Admiral Pownall: These admirals would come aboard. I'd meet them up there at the gangway, and they'd go down into the cabin. It eventually came out that Kimmel would relieve him. I was not a great admirer of Kimmel's, but that's the way it was.

Q: Did you talk to Admiral Richardson about the situation? Did you have any conversations?

Admiral Pownall: No. He was very close-mouthed about anything like that. I was his captain.

Mrs. Pownall: So much so, that after he got back he never said a word. We found out afterward He gave Charles a copy of a letter--he had an old maid schoolteacher. She wrote to him and said, "J. O., you have had a wonderful experience. This has been a dreadful thing for you, but don't talk about it."

He said, "I made up my mind, I wasn't ever going to say anything about it." And he didn't, he kept his mouth absolutely shut.*

---

*Richardson finally broke the silence with the publication of a revealing memoir, On the Treadmill to Pearl Harbor (Washington, D. C.: U. S. Government Printing Office, 1973).

Admiral Pownall: She also said that, "You might have been playing the other part, and the other fellow playing your part."

In other words, he could have been in the President's place and the President could have been in his place.

Q: Admiral George Dyer, I believe this is correct, has interviewed Admiral Richardson and apparently is going to release a book of his memoirs, when Admiral Richardson is no longer living.* That's my understanding. It should be interesting. I admire Admiral Dyer very much.

Admiral Pownall: I remember on the Enterprise when J. O. said he was going to use it as his flagship, we built a cage for the enlarged office inside of his cabin. I think George Dyer was in on that. The commander in chief has a big staff, so we accommodated them. Admiral Taffinder was chief of staff.**

Q: He was my first admiral that I ever knew.

Admiral Pownall: I kept a box of cigars for him in my cabin.

---

*Vice Admiral George C. Dyer, USN (Ret.), was Richardson's collaborator for On the Treadmill to Pearl Harbor.
**Captain Sherwoode A. Taffinder, USN, later a rear admiral.

Q: Wonderful person to me.

Admiral Pownall: He'd come over, and he knew I had this box of cigars. He liked to talk to me, too. I purposely put the box of cigars out where he could have one while we were talking, Sherwoode Taffinder.

Q: It must have been a tense situation when you were out there. You were aware of the possibilities, of course.

Admiral Pownall: True, almost at war.

Q: Do you remember any alerts or any feeling that war was imminent? Do you have any recollections of this time?

Admiral Pownall: We were on alert most of the time. We were over at Lahaina Roads. We were over there and at Honolulu. We took on a warlike attitude at sea then. We knew there was something up, and we had to be careful.

Q: Do you think the fleet was as unprepared as the general public has been given the impression that it was?

Admiral Pownall: No. On the _Enterprise_, we had our guns manned in the evening and in the early morning. That's

Pownall #1 - 104

about all we could do. We were ready if they did come.

Of course, at the attack on Pearl Harbor, I wasn't there.

Q: What about the planes, what was their operation?

Admiral Pownall: We operated mostly gunnery and nav hops. Of course, you had to do a lot of flying to keep the kids in on landings and takeoffs.

Q: Were they doing any scouting or patrolling or search operations?

Admiral Pownall: Yes, we searched.

I went from the Enterprise to Norfolk.

Q: Commanding officer of the Naval Air Station, Naval Operating Base at Norfolk and became a rear admiral at that time.

Admiral Pownall: Yes, they made me a rear admiral.

Q: What year was that, '41 or '42?

Admiral Pownall: It was '42, but they put it back to the third of December before the strike. They did that with all those men that were selected at that time.

Q: What were you doing at Pearl Harbor time? Do you remember the specific time, and your reactions, and what happened that day?

Admiral Pownall: I was in Norfolk, as captain of the naval air station.

Mrs. Pownall: You were taking an afternoon nap. It was Sunday afternoon.

Admiral Pownall: I always thought they would hit the Philippines instead.

Mrs. Pownall: I remember I woke you up and said the radio message had come that Pearl Harbor had been hit. And you said, "Oh, you don't mean Pearl Harbor."

Admiral Pownall: That was the first time we had a good government house to live in, as captain of the air station.

Mrs. Pownall: That was the first time we'd ever had quarters.

Q: Yes, sure. Every other time you'd been either at sea

or in Washington. But you were only there a year. Can you tell me something about that duty?

Admiral Pownall: During that year, Adolphus Andrews came down to Norfolk and said, "Things are serious on this coast.* German submarines are sinking all our tankers, and we can't get oil to New England. And now our inland waterways are not very good. We haven't any more barges, and we're not prepared. We should be prepared with inland waterways and all that sort of thing to take place of the tankers that are being sunk by the Germans out there, on your coast incidentally."

I was one of those called in to see if we could think of something. I solved one thing--it was to put a light on a destroyer. One thing, I guess, you fly all night and may get vertigo in looking at a compass and all that. I didn't want any of my kids to get vertigo. So I thought of this idea and tried it out--of putting a vertical light showing red, that showed up. Not horizontally, because you couldn't have a red light showing horizontal. That would be a point of reference for the patrol planes. Then my patrol planes, from the air station, could orient on this destroyer, and we'd go out and try to find the submarines. It sounded all right, and it seemed all right.

---
*By that time Andrews had reverted from vice admiral to rear admiral and was serving as Commandant of the Third Naval District and Commander North Atlantic Coastal Frontier.

Then I moved my office over to my bedroom, so I'd be ready to operate at night in my quarters. We went to bed that night, and ding-a-ling about 2:00 o'clock--"We got one."

I said, "How do you know you got one?"

He said, "The Roper's returning to port tomorrow with 29 dead Germans."*

The thing had worked. The Roper came up on this fellow, and he was on the surface. He had been located by a plane, and also by the destroyer. The Roper put it on him, and they jumped overboard. The shock from the depth charges killed them, and the submarine sank right there.

So we didn't have much of a funeral. We had 29 dead Germans. I said, "The naval air station will try to fill the hangar, but the supply department has got to empty it."

That aroused the supply officer and he said, "I'll bury the bastards."

I said, "No, we're not going to do it. I don't have the trucks to do it." The commandant backed me up.

They buried them in the Hampton cemetery, in Phoebus. It's a military cemetery.

Q: So your idea had been successful.

---

*The USS Roper (DD-147) became the first U. S. naval vessel to sink a U-boat during World War II. Her victim, on the night of 13-14 April 1942, was the U-85. For an account see Samuel E. Morison, The Battle of the Atlantic, 1939-1943 (Boston: Little, Brown, 1947), page 155.

Admiral Pownall: I don't know, but that was the beginning of antisubmarine warfare. At least, we started then from that.

Mrs. Pownall: After Charles was relieved, these boys that he had put on this thing got another one. Did they sink that one?

Admiral Pownall: They sunk it. I made a statement that anyone that got a submarine got a case of champagne.

Mary stayed back. I was sent out to the West Coast. She sent me a message, "You owe another case of champagne." The Coast Guard got it, from Elizabeth City. They were under me.

Q: Do I understand that by doing this particular arrangement of lights on a destroyer, that was the beginning of antisubmarine warfare?

Admiral Pownall: I think so.

Q: Planes and destroyers working together?

Admiral Pownall: Nothing has ever been said about it,

because Admiral King put top secret on everything about it.* Nobody was allowed to say anything. No medals or anything, except that we did get a Navy Cross for the captain of the Roper.

Q: This was the first beginning of the working together of the plane-destroyer combination that did work out to be successful?

Admiral Pownall: That's right. You hit it right on the head.

Q: That's interesting. I'd never heard that.

---

*In December 1941 Admiral Ernest J. King, USN, had become Commander in Chief U. S. Fleet.

Interview Number 2 with Vice Admiral Charles A. Pownall,
U. S. Navy (Retired, and Mrs. Mary Pownall

Place: The Pownalls' home in La Jolla, California

Date: Sunday, 12 April 1970

Interviewer: Commander Etta-Belle Kitchen, U. S. Navy (Retired)


Q: I think, Admiral, that we talked after the end of the tape yesterday and realized that there were many interesting things about your duty in Norfolk that maybe we hadn't put on the tape. I'm sure that you can go ahead this morning and add some more interesting items.

Admiral Pownall: Back in Norfolk--the commandant called me up one morning and said, "The Prime Minister and party are coming in on the <u>Duke of York</u>.* He has to go to Washington right away and meet with the President. Will you look out for him? Will you get him up there?"

The <u>Duke of York</u> was anchored out in the roads. I only had one plane, an old TC-3, and one pilot, because it took me all of a sudden. We got him in and . . .

Q: You haven't said his name yet.

Admiral Pownall: Winston Churchill.

---
*The <u>Duke of York</u> was a British battleship, just completed in November 1941. She was the third ship of the <u>King George V</u> class.

Pownall #2 - 111

When he got in the station and went on out to the big field there, he made this statement. He said, "What fools they are to think they can knock down a nation that can build things like this." That's true.

Q: What was he speaking about?

Admiral Pownall: The field at Norfolk. It's a slab of concrete on a swamp. Instead of filling up the swamp, they just put concrete on top of it. And that's the field at Norfolk.

Q: What is the name of that field?

Admiral Pownall: I forget now. It was named for an early day pilot. The station field was Bellinger.

Q: Who went out to get him?

Admiral Pownall: I didn't go out to get him, but I was there when they sent a launch out. They had a big party.
   We called it "Operation Ham." They all got hams, or creates of oranges, or nylons. They wanted to take stockings back.
   Finally I went to say that, "The engines of planes had

no regard for rank. And we could just load them so much and no more. Couldn't we please send the baggage separate from the passengers?"

The answer came back from the Embassy, "The baggage will accompany their respective passengers."

I had to rehearse this business. We had old Clipper planes, British Clippers, too. I had to use a sailing launch to load the planes. Fortunately we had one that would fit right in the sub of the wing. So we were all ready for that.

I said to the Prime Minister, "Sir, I'm sorry I can't get that baggage here in time for your dinner with the President." And this to me, he looked at his cuffs and said, "Oh, this shirt's all right. Don't worry."

Q: He put emphasis on the right things.
Who flew him up, do you remember? You didn't go with him?

Admiral Pownall: I forget his name now. I didn't go with him.

When he came back, he came back on a train. We brought the train right into the air station.

I had orders to have him in the air by 11:30, or something like that. I had everything loaded in time, except the Prime Minister.

So I went back to the train. It was in the back of the station there, and ran into his valet. He said, "Oh, I'll have him up in a minute. He had a hard night last night."

Q: He was still in bed?

Admiral Pownall: Yes. We got him off on time.

Mrs. Pownall: Did you tell about their coming in? That was a great surprise; nobody knew he was coming in. Did you say about all that group that came before that? We had no idea why they were there, French aviators and people like that.

Q: He said he had a large party with him, but he didn't indicate there was a pre-group.

Mrs. Pownall: Yes, there was, because we had that party for them.

Admiral Pownall: The red, white, and blues were his party. The white was Beaverbrook, he had the press.* The blue was the Navy, which was Dudley Pound.** I think we gave

---
*William Maxwell Aitken, Lord Beaverbrook, was a well-known British newspaper publisher.
**Admiral of the Fleet Sir Alfred Dudley Pound, RN, First Sea Lord, 1939-43.

Pownall #2 - 114

Winston Churchill the color red. So it was a red, white, and blue thing. We had tagged it all, and that's the way we could manage it.

Q: He's explained that they flew up and then returned by train.

Admiral Pownall: That was interesting. They flew from Norfolk to Bermuda.

Q: He didn't go back aboard his ship?

Admiral Pownall: No, he flew back to Bermuda, then from Bermuda to the British Isles.

Mrs. Pownall: We also had the Bermuda Governor and his wife visit us.
    What I thought also was so interesting was those four British carriers that came in.

Q: Can you tell me about that, Admiral?

Admiral Pownall: We became a repair base, at the Norfolk Navy Yard, for Allied carriers. Of course, the British have funny names for theirs--<u>Invulnerable</u>, <u>Indomitable</u>,

Illustrious. They came in and had their planes over at the air station.

One thing was that one of our little fighter boys taxied into a Hurricane plane.* His squadron commander gave him an "Iron Cross." Fortunately, we had enough spares that we could fix it, but it was a rather delicate moment.

Q: Yes, I can see that it might be.

Admiral Pownall: And also one other thing, this, to American aircraft carriers, means "You're high."**

Q: The admiral is gesturing with his arms, lifting them in the air.

Admiral Pownall: And this means "you're too low."

Q: Putting his arms down.

Admiral Pownall: With the British, it was just the opposite.

I said, "Well, you'll have to come around to our way, or you won't get trained." We had to keep training them.

---
*The Hurricane was a British fighter plane.
**This was a signal to the approaching pilot from the landing signal officer at the after end of an aircraft carrier's flight deck.

Pownall #2 - 116

That was one time the British gave way to American aviation and followed our ruling. But right after it was over, they went back to their old way.

Q: You spoke of doing training. Were you training British pilots?

Admiral Pownall: Yes.

Mrs. Pownall: There in Norfolk, they were out of their training, because the ship was tied up.

Q: While the ship was there you were doing the training.

So that was another feature of your job that would not be in the ordinary course of events.

Mrs. Pownall: Also about Mountbatten taking over.*

Admiral Pownall: The civilian airport in Norfolk is way out in the country; it's very difficult. Here was Lord Louis Mountbatten and he wanted to go to New York on British business. They'd had a ruling that we were to stop flying the British around.

---
*Captain Louis Mountbatten, RN, was designated commanding officer of the aircraft carrier Illustrious while she was undergoing repairs at the Norfolk Navy Yard, but he was promoted to flag rank and relieved before the ship returned to sea.

I didn't have the heart to have Mountbatten go all the way out to that civilian airport. So I called up the Navy Department and said, "Unless I have positive orders, I'm going to fly Mountbatten to New York." I thought I was getting my neck out, but Admiral King, God bless him, said later, "You did the right thing."

It was a youngster in CNO that had issued this order against the British.

Q: I was going to ask you something of that background-- what was the basis for issuing this order? Had they been taking advantage of our hospitalities?

Admiral Pownall: I guess so, but not in Norfolk.

We had supplied transports. Sometimes you had to shut down on congressmen and others that want too much. And this was a similar case.

Q: The stories of the British when they first came over when they were in dire straits, and the procedures they followed when we actually were redoing ships for them--you probably are aware of that.

Mrs. Pownall: This _Illustrious_ had a hole the whole way through her. The captain lost all his dress uniforms.

Pownall #2 - 118

When he came ashore and stayed with us, all he had to wear was shorts like the British wear. He even went out to dinner with us with these shorts on. He just didn't have any uniforms.

Q: In those days I couldn't think of anything really less important, and I'm sure they felt the same way.

Mrs. Pownall: Everybody felt that way about these people. They didn't have any uniforms. All their mess attendants were killed; it was that section.

Q: You haven't told me yet about the "Battenberg Cup." You have a picture here of receiving it. Battenberg, I believe, was the grandfather of Mountbatten. That was what brought it to my attention.

Admiral Pownall: Yes, that's right.

Mrs. Pownall: That, of course, was on the _Enterprise_.

Q: Can you refer back to your time on the _Enterprise_? The reason I do it is that Admiral Sabin has mentioned the "Battenberg Cup," and that you had the picture of your receiving it.

Pownall #2 - 119

Admiral Pownall: I told you that Kelly, a coxswain, was an oarsman on the California. I had said that if the crew wanted a race boat, the captain certainly did and so did the exec. So Kelly came up later and said that the crew wanted a race boat. They got it and trained.

We went to San Francisco. Later we rowed against the battleships and we won. We won both at San Francisco and against the battle fleet at Guantanamo. We won the cup the second time.

This [referring to the picture] is when we lost it. This is the West Virginia who won it, and we're presenting it to them.

Sabin was the athletic officer on the West Virginia.*

Q: That's why he remembers it so well.

Mrs. Pownall: He had that cup for a while.

Q: Yes, I think he did. In fact, I think his name was the last one inscribed on it.

He had it and it was in his quarters when Lord Mountbatten came to visit him, and he was most interested

---

*From 1940 to 1942, Lieutenant Commander Lorenzo S. Sabin, Jr., USN, served on the staff of Commander Battleships Battle Force, embarked in the West Virginia (BB-48).

in seeing it.*

Admiral Pownall: I can tell you another thing--we won the sailing race, too, not with a rowboat but with a sailing boat. Claude Bloch was our admiral.** He called me over on board his flagship, and I thought I'd done something. He said, "I want to congratulate you and the carrier, your ship, for putting those cruisers straight. Here comes an aircraft carrier and beats the cruisers in rowing and in sailing. And I just want to congratulate you." He had a lot of humor in him.

Q: That was when you were on the <u>Enterprise</u>?

Admiral Pownall: Yes.
   I was detached from Norfolk in May.

Q: I have May '42 you left. That was a very interesting period of your career, wasn't it, the Norfolk assignment?

Admiral Pownall: Oh, yes. It was a good command, nice people. The old South.

Q: I have May '42, that would have been more than a year, that you were Commander Patrol Plane Replacement Squadron--

---

*Mountbatten visited Pearl Harbor in 1941 while the <u>Illustrious</u> was being repaired.
**Admiral Claude C. Bloch, USN, served as Comander in Chief U. S. Fleet, 1938-40.

Patrol Wings Pacific Fleet, then Commander Fleet Air West Coast. Where was this?

Admiral Pownall: At Coronado.

Q: Now you were there for a year and three months. That was in the early days of the war, of course. Can you tell me something of your experiences there?

Admiral Pownall: One thing, yes--I know we had those patrol planes. The Coronado had just come out, she was a big patrol plane.* I went out on her trials. The thought was: "Is this the Navy's future in bombing?"--big bombers, because the Coronado had the gliding characteristics of a ten-ton truck.

Q: Like a rock?

Admiral Pownall: Yes.
 To make a long story short--we succeeded in making a deal with the Air Force that we'd get one out of every ten of the B-24s.** We wanted the B-24 to take the Coronado's place. So we had to give up the production from one firm,

---
*The Consolidated PB2Y first reached a fleet squadron in December 1940.
**When the Consolidated B-24s were turned over to the Navy, they got the designation PB4Y.

and for that we got--one out of every ten was a B-24. We had promised them to Admiral Fitch; he wanted them down at Guadalcanal.*

The Consolidated people, with old Tom Girdler as chairman, we contracted to train one crew or maybe two crews.** And then we'd have to train our own. We finally got out to Camp Pendleton.*** We had a field up at Camp Pendleton and trained our own crews after Consolidated had trained one.

The only thing was we had to make a lot of changes because the Navy's version had more radio and other things. I think we had to put an extra section in the middle of the plane. We just did meet our date for Admiral Fitch at Guadalcanal for these B-24s.

Q: How many did you send him, do you remember?

Admiral Pownall: I forget now.

Q: But he sure needed them.

Admiral Pownall: He sure needed them.

That was the beginning of the end of the Navy's patrol

---

*Rear Admiral Aubrey W. Fitch, USN, Commander Air South Pacific.
**Tom M. Girdler was chairman of the board of the Consolidated Vultee Aircraft Corporation.
***Camp Pendleton is a Marine Corps base in Southern California.

planes. We took the land type plane, the B-24s.

Q: What was Consolidated training them for?

Admiral Pownall: Consolidated was making them for the Air Force, the B-24s.

Q: And they were training Air Force pilots?

Admiral Pownall: No. Of course, they had their own test crews. We just took one of their test crews to teach our crew how to fly a B-24. After we got one crew trained, we could train another crew. We used Camp Pendleton. They had one place that was big enough, not too big, and you had to come over a sort of hill to get into it. That's the beginning of the demise of the old seaplane.

Admiral Nimitz came to San Francisco and wanted to see me. He and McCormick, his chief of staff, came up to San Francisco and took me to lunch, I remember.* They wanted to talk about moving our headquarters to San Francisco. Nimitz was from San Francisco, and he sort of liked that area. I told him, "No."

A little while later I was ordered out to . . .

---
*Captain Lynde D. McCormick, USN, Pacific Fleet war plans officer.

Pownall #2 - 124

Q: Let me just interrupt--did you think that he was displeased with your not agreeing with him?

Admiral Pownall: No, he wasn't that kind. He didn't want any yes-men in this outfit.

Q: You weren't implying that because you didn't agree with him that then you were detached from one job and sent to another?

Admiral Pownall: No.

Q: Can you tell me a little about that meeting with Admiral Nimitz, expand on that a little bit more? Where did you go for lunch, for example?

Admiral Pownall: One thing--that was a patrol plane, and it made a bad landing. McCormick was hurt a little bit and Nimitz was shook up.*

Q: You mean when they came into San Francisco?

Admiral Pownall: To land, yes. We went out to dinner; I forget where we went. I can't remember what we talked about.

---

*This incident, which occurred 30 June 1942, is covered in Potter's Nimitz, pages 109-111.

Within a week, I was ordered out as Commander Carrier Division Three.

Q: So the answer was he was most favorably impressed with you, or he wouldn't have ordered you out to forward duty.

Admiral Pownall: I don't know.

Mary can tell you about the time he came to San Diego--this was earlier--I had the mumps.

Mrs. Pownall: Charles had been going around inspecting these different air bases. They had mumps on one of them; they were having a regular epidemic. When he came back, he came down with the mumps. He had a really bad case, and we had to keep him in bed.

Admiral Nimitz from the Pacific came and Admiral King from Washington came, and we gave a party for them. Charles was in bed and I said, "You're not going to get up and go down and see the admirals, because I think it would be terrible." He said he was going to. So he did, he came down to the party.

It came out that he had had the mumps and should have been in bed. Charles said to Nimitz, "Admiral, I'm awfully sorry about this. I hope that you have had the mumps."

He said, "No, I haven't."

Charles said, "My face will be red."

He said, "There will be something else red, if I get the mumps."

Q: That was rather a historic occasion, having both of them come and be at your quarters.

Admiral Pownall: Yes. They did that all the time. San Diego became a sort of a meeting place.

Q: I knew that he came in rather frequently to see Admiral King in San Francisco, but I did not know that both of them came also to San Diego.

Admiral Pownall: I don't know that they came very often, but they did this time.

Q: Do you remember when that was, admiral? Was it during this tour?

Mrs. Pownall: Yes. That was the reason they were there for this conference, of course, my husband was part of it.

Q: Do you know what the conference was about?

Admiral Pownall: That's a long time ago.

Q: So many of these things, now with writing the biography, haven't been put in history. Those tiny incidents make for interest.

If you were ill, you probably weren't in on the conference.

Admiral Pownall: I wasn't, no.

But I had permission from the doctor. I didn't deliberately expose two leading naval officers to mumps. I don't have that on my record.

Q: I wouldn't think so, because that would be a matter of judgment really, and you would not take that chance.

Admiral Pownall: At that time it was whether a carrier was ready, when ships became operative, how many pilots we could turn out, and our training. It was the general logistic setup that concerned both Nimitz and King at the conference.

I said that we were training the wrong way. We'd have to save Sunday for funerals, particularly when we came out to the West Coast.

What we were doing was to take a less trained pilot and put him in the fastest and heaviest airplane, and land him on the smallest carrier in the worst ocean. No wonder we killed them.

That didn't rest well on a certain four-star man. He never forgave me for that.

Q: Is this Nimitz?

Admiral Pownall: No, King.

Q: You told King. What did you recommend as a difference?

Admiral Pownall: I recommended that they put a carrier in the Gulf of Mexico. When a boy was hot, in a light plane, land him on the carrier, where he could just wiggle that plane around, and he had a lot of deck, and he didn't have to worry too much about the ocean. Because we'd had cases where these boys from Nebraska, brought up in the cornfields, were excellent pilots, but when it came to landing on a carrier, they'd stiffen up.

So that's what my point was. So eventually I was ordered back to train pilots.

Q: Yes, I know, later you were. Then they did follow your advice?

Admiral Pownall: Yes.

Q: It seems really so simple.

Admiral Pownall: First they had the <u>Guadalcanal</u>, when I was Chief of Training. Then they put a larger carrier in. The <u>Guadalcanal</u> was a five and ten store carrier, a jeep carrier.

Q: I'm glad you told Admiral King that. You were having a very high casualty rate, you say.

Admiral Pownall: Yes.
We'd have them at San Diego before they'd go out to the fleet. We had to do that work, and it should have been done before they came out there.

Q: I would think the high mortality would have been extremely bad psychology for the pilots.

Admiral Pownall: When you're young, you forget those things.
The chapel, when I was in patrol squadrons, was right next door to our office, so I remember that very distinctly.

Q: That must not have been a happy situation for you.

Admiral Pownall: Now I'm Commander Carrier Division Three. I flew out and landed. I'd have liked to have had the Lexington with Felix Stump for my flagship, but they decreed that I'd have the Yorktown with Jock Clark.* Then they said, "You can exchange. Take one ship one time, and one the other." So that's the way it ended.

Q: You flew to Pearl, and then who made your assignment?

Admiral Pownall: Admiral Nimitz.

Q: Did you talk to Admiral Nimitz then?

Admiral Pownall: Yes.

Q: What did he say?

Admiral Pownall: He was always the same; he was gracious and nice. We'd been friends a long time.

I was ordered to go out to Marcus.

One thing Nimitz said, "I'm going to give you a battleship. You may run into something out there." He gave me the Indiana with Bill Fechteler in command.**

---

*Captain Felix B. Stump, USN; Captain Joseph J. Clark, USN.
**Captain William M. Fechteler, USN, who served as Vice Chief of Naval Operations, as an admiral, from 1951 to 1953.

He said, "Don't try to win the war all at once, because you don't have enough oil. That tanker that you're taking is all the oil west of Pearl for the carriers." That was a warning.

Then I thought, "If I get a kid down out there, how am I going to pick him up?" I went to Charlie Lockwood and said, "How about using a submarine to rescue in case I have a pilot down?"*

He said, "I'll talk it over with Nimitz, but I think it will be all right. I don't know whether I can get one out there to Marcus or not."

That was the start of the Lifeguard League. It's in his book.** They picked up 500 pilots.

Q: But did you go with Admiral Lockwood to see Admiral Nimitz about this?

Admiral Pownall: No, we went separately.

Then we sailed for Marcus. My flagship was the Yorktown with Jock Clark in command. Then I had with me a battleship, the Indiana, and some cruisers and destroyers. I had quite a force.

The thing to do is catch them when they don't expect

---
*Vice Admiral Charles A. Lockwood, Jr., USN, Commander Submarines Pacific Fleet.
**Lockwood's book is Sink 'Em All: Submarine Warfare in the Pacific (New York: E. P. Dutton, 1951): See pages 119-120.

you. You do the damage and get out of there without losing anybody. We lost one aviator I think, but he was captured and taken prisoner.

Q: And you were at that time commanding officer of Task Force 15 for the Marcus operation.

Admiral Pownall: I was administratively Carrier Division Three. I had the Yorktown, Essex, and Lexington.

Q: Tell me about that. You said you lost one. But what happened? Of course, I know you can't see what's going on. You're too far away, but you know about it, I'm sure.

Admiral Pownall: It was a success. Our intelligence officer said it was quite a success. I remember we killed quite a few Japs, and they never used Marcus after that. It sort of wiped off the battle business with the Japs.

Q: It was one annoyance you didn't have to worry about anymore.

Admiral Pownall: It was supposed to be a training operation as well, just to see whether we could do it or not. And it worked out all right.

Q: Let me take the time now to read the commendation that Admiral Nimitz wrote for you concerning the Marcus Island carrier air strike on 1 September 1943. It says:

"A carrier striking force under your command executed an air attack on Marcus Island on 1 September 1943. The highly satisfactory results of this attack have been fully attested by photographs taken during the course of the action.

"I have reviewed the statement of intentions and the detailed plans which you prepared for this operation. I find these papers to be a full and thorough appreciation of the mission with which you were charged and the means of its execution. This was an essential preface to so fine a success.

"I commend you for the excellent planning and the excellent accomplishment of the subject mission."

Then he says that a copy of this will go in your personnel file. I've read many commendations, but I've never read that particular paragraph about the excellent pre-planning, which to me would be essential to any job.

Mrs. Pownall: He was always noted for his planning, just like I told you about the Saratoga, going down the river and taking all that. He's always done that.

Admiral Pownall: Soc McMorris put that in.* He was on the staff there.

Q: Obviously, Admiral Nimitz didn't dictate it. Somebody who knew you put it in. But I think it's noteworthy, because we all know that the success of anything is measured by the planning that went ahead.

Then you went back to Pearl.

Admiral Pownall: Back to Pearl and was immediately ordered to go to Tarawa, to hit Tarawa. Also they gave me two light cruisers that had been converted to carriers. One was Mel Pride, and the other was George Henderson commanding.** So as soon as we could, we went again.

We hit Tarawa, killed the commanding officer of Tarawa, a Jap. Which was a mistake because the next one was a worse one. His relief turned out to be a civil engineer who specialized in pillboxes. That's the reason that Tarawa became such a terrible place. They killed a lot of good Marines.

I didn't get credit for a good job at Tarawa until later, when we found out that we had done more than we thought we had. But that's neither here nor there.

---
*Rear Admiral Charles H. McMorris.
**Captain Alfred M. Pride, USN, commanding officer of the USS Belleau Wood (CVL-24); Captain George R. Henderson, USN, commanding officer of the USS Princeton (CVL-23). Pride's oral history is in the Naval Institute collection.

We came back from Tarawa and I changed over to the Lexington.

Q: Tarawa was in the Gilberts in November of '43, I believe.

Admiral Pownall: I think we made a second strike down in that area. I know I was on the Lexington, with Felix Stump who was the captain. We were trying to get in there quietly so the Japs wouldn't know we were coming.

A phosphorus bomb on one of our ships dropped on the flight deck. Thank goodness, it was parked on the outer rim, or we would have had one of those terrific aircraft fires. So we just pushed the plane over the side. We thought, of course, since we had lighted up the sky, that we'd have unwelcome visitors. But we got in all right. I think that was Tarawa again.

When we hit the Gilberts, we had four task forces. The one had the job of backing up the Marines at Tarawa; I didn't.

I took one up, as the citation said, to keep Mili down.

Mrs. Pownall: Which was the one you got the DSO?*

---
*DSO--Distinguished Service Order.

Admiral Pownall: It was a big task force. I took the one up and intercepted, nearest the enemy I guess you'd say, which is where the commanding officer should be. We had to keep Mili down.

One thing that's interesting--Charlie Crommelin was one of my squadron commanders.* We were going into see how well we had hit Mili and how much more bombs we needed to put on Mili. I wouldn't send the scouts unless they had fighter protection.

Charlie had just been flying and he said, "Admiral, may I go in, because you're using some of my fighters, and I'd like to lead the operation for the strike. I'd like to see about those blankety-blanks on the ground."

I sensed something right then. I said, "Charlie, you're going to go down and try to get hurt. I don't want you riding down just to knock out one. They're pretty good."

He said, "No, sir. I raise my right hand and swear to you that I will not, but I just want to see."

So I said, "Okay." So they went in.

It wasn't very much longer, when, "Please clear the flight deck. Crommelin is coming back and has to come right aboard. He can't take a waveoff." Charlie came in and landed. He got out of the plane and then fainted.

---

*Lieutenant Commander Charles L. Crommelin, USN, Commander Air Group Five in the USS Yorktown (CV-10), Pownall's flagship.

He went to sick bay. When he got in sick bay he told the corpsman to please get word to the admiral that he didn't disobey orders.

What had happened--the Japs had started using shrapnel. All they had to do was get the bullet in the cockpit, and then it would explode. Charlie had powder marks all over his body. This was Tarawa.

I was up in Mili, the islands north.

Q: And he wanted to go down and see what was going on at Tarawa.

Admiral Pownall: Yes. We had that job, to keep those planes from those places from interfering with our landing operation. This was different from Marcus. We didn't have any landing there. But Tarawa was a landing operation. When you have a landing operation to do, it's a little more than just go in and strike and get out.

I knew that the Japs had pretty good gunnery. Also it was their idea if you hit them once, you're not going to hit them again right away. We'd lose more on the second attack. That's the reason I used the element of surprise as much as possible; it pays off.

We're in the Gilberts operation now. I had Task Force 15.

Pownall #2 - 138

Q: I have 15 for Marcus, Gilbert, and the first Tarawa.

Then, later, on the landing, you were commanding Task Force 50. Is that correct?

Admiral Pownall: Yes, I guess it was. I had more ships then.

I prided myself on the Gilberts business, because we got a "well done" from the admiral for that. It was also the first time that I know of we intercepted enemy planes in the air, and then vectored our own fighters out directly against them and shot them down. I think that was the first time we'd done that, so I felt pretty good about that. And we didn't lose many kids.

Q: This was when you were with Felix Stump?

Admiral Pownall: Yes, he was my old exec in the Enterprise.

Mrs. Pownall: This wonderful decoration from the British is for the Gilberts.

Admiral Pownall: The British DSO.

The Gilberts are British islands, had been and are now. They have been returned; Britain still owns them.

Q: You were with Jock Clark, and, of course, he is kind of a colorful guy. Did you have any anecdotes concerning him that are worthy, or of Admiral Stump, either one that you can relate?

Admiral Pownall: I was devoted to Stump. Jock and I didn't always see each other.

This time both of them were involved--when the Liscome Bay was sunk. We had just finished flying for the day, and were going to go out and fuel. All of a sudden on a dark night, there were three airplanes overhead. The Lexington was rigged for morning takeoff, all her planes were aft ready to go. I told Jock to take them aboard.

One came down on the Liscome Bay. They had no place to go. He didn't do well, and he went through the barrier and into the planes and set them on fire and killed five men. The flight deck was out of commission.

Jock said, "Admiral, may I go down below and work on that flight deck?" He was so energetic, he wasn't satisfied with what they were doing down there. The captain's place is on the bridge, but Jock wanted to go down, and I let him go.

He had his good points. He's a four-star admiral now. He outranks me.*

---

*Both Pownall and Clark were advanced one rank upon retirement on the basis of combat awards.

Q: He's written a book.*

Mrs. Pownall: That book has certainly caused an awful lot of controversy.

Q: Much comment, to say the least.

Admiral Pownall: I don't read those. The war is over. I hope I'm not adding fuel to the fire.

One thing--we had the second plane in the air and no place for him to go. The Lexington moved the planes off the arresting gear as fast as they could. Felix had his landing signal officer talk with the pilot, this youngster--how much gas he had. Of course, the kid had to make one pass; he only had about a pint of gasoline left. But we got him in and saved his life.

With the other boy, who had killed five, we thought they both should go back to flying and get this out of their heads. They both turned out well.

We had a funeral on the flight deck of the Yorktown. We had both Catholic and Protestant chaplains.**

Also, we had another one on Jock's, one of the mess boys. He said, "I ain't been ordained, but I can

---

*Joseph J. Clark, Carrier Admiral (New York: McKay, 1967).
**Father Walter S. Farrell, S.J., a noted theological scholar; Presbyterian Robert L. Alexander of Lumberton, North Carolina.

preach.*

I asked him later, "How are you doing with your preaching?"

"Well," he said, "I think there's less cussing, but the sins of the flesh are still there."

Q: This was one of the Negro mess boys?

Admiral Pownall: Yes.

Q: You have two citations that I want to read, and maybe they will trigger your memory on some other incidents.

One is on the Yorktown and covers the period from '43 to '45, and the other one is the Distinguished Service Medal.

I think I'll read the Presidential Unit Citation first on the Yorktown. It says:

"For extraordinary heroism in action against enemy Japanese forces in the air, at sea, and on shore in the Pacific war area from August 31st, 1943 to August 15th, 1945. Spearheading our concentrated carrier warfare in forward areas, the Yorktown and her air group struck crushing blows toward annihilating the enemy's fighting strength. Daring and dependable in combat, she, with her gallant officers and men, rendered loyal service in

---

*"Brother" Davenport of West Point, Mississippi.

achieving the ultimate defeat of the Japanese Empire."

Admiral Pownall: That's the Presidential Unit Citation. I don't have that. I have the little ribbon, but not the written citation. That came from the Yorktown. I guess Jock never sent it to me. It was for the whole ship.

Q: Then the Distinguished Medal reads:

"For exceptionally meritorious and distinguished service to the government of the United States in a duty of great responsibility as a task force commander of the Central Pacific Force, during the seizure and occupation of the Gilbert Islands in November, and later as Commander of the task force which raided the Marshall Islands in December of '43, maintaining control of the air throughout the entire period. He later directed vigorous attacks against enemy aircraft, shipping, and shore emplacements which culminated in the successful completion of each hazardous assignment."

Now we haven't talked about the Marshall yet, have we?

Admiral Pownall: No, we didn't go to the Marshalls until after we'd had the Gilberts.

Mrs. Pownall: Now this one I love because it sounds like Pinafore. That's by the King.

Q: This other citation is January '45. We're getting a little ahead of ourselves, but it relates to a previous period.

This is for the operations in the Gilbert Islands, and it's dated 18 January '45:

"Sir, I am commanded by my Lords Commissioners of the Admiralty to inform you that they have learned with great pleasure that on the advice of the First Lord, the King has been graciously pleased to approve your honorary appointment as a Companion of the Distinguished Service Order for outstanding gallantry and leadership shown as commander of the Carrier Force, Central Pacific Force, in the operations for the reconquest of the Gilbert Islands.

"The insignia will be presented to you in due course. I am, Sir, your obedient servant, H. V. Markham."

To Rear Admiral Charles A. Pownall, D.S.O., USN.

I have also an impressive manuscript from the King. It has in the upper righthand corner, written in longhand, "George R. I." It reads:

"George the VI, by the grace of God, Great Britain, Ireland, and the British Dominions beyond the seas, King, defender of the Faith, Emperor of India, Sovereign of the Distinguished Service Order, to Charles Allan Pownall, Rear Admiral in the United States Navy.

"Greetings, whereas we have thought fit to nominate

and appoint you to be an honorary member of our Distinguished Service Order, we do by these presents grant unto you the dignity of an honorary of companion of our said order and we do hereby authorize you to have, hold, and enjoy the said dignity as an honorary member of our said order, together with all and singular the privileges thereupon belonging or appertaining.

"Given at our Court at St. James's, under our signed manual, this 11th day of January 1945 in the ninth year of our reign. By the sovereign's command, signed Hall, First Lord of the Admiralty."

Q: That certainly is flowery language, isn't it?

Admiral Pownall: The British are good at that.

Q: Yes, they are. They've been doing it for a long time.
    I want you to be sure that you've covered the items that come to your mind concerning Tarawa and the Gilberts, before we go on to the Marshalls.

Admiral Pownall: I wish I'd had a helicopter. I had a submarine and they helped out in rescuing any that were shot down.

Q: You were in that particular area until 1944?

Admiral Pownall: That's right.

For the Marshalls, then they changed our task force. They took the battleships away and gave me cruisers. Also we had to refuel. I had to go up to the north of the Marshalls.

The kids were pretty tired after the Gilberts. You can't just get them well by turning them in their bunks. We had to relax some place.

As expressed by some of them, it's like the Army-Navy game. Then on the way back to Annapolis, you'd stop off at Baltimore and play the Giants.

One thing--I was not enthusiastic about the Marshalls. Because the kids, with all due respect, should get ashore. The submarines had made it quite a point of relaxation that way. They had a place where they could get ashore and get into a bathing suit and get it out of their system.

Just like a football team; carrier pilots are a good bit like an athletic team, you have to catch them when they're up. They have to be in good condition, and their airplane has to be in good condition, or you'll have lots of losses.

We had orders to go up to the north part of the Marshalls, refuel, and at night. I had a hard time doing that, too, because there were a lot of ships up there. It was dark, and we had to operate by radar.

Pownall #2 - 146

My nickname, of course, was "Baldy." Ted Sherman was "Ted."* We'd start the message, "Ted to Baldy. Will you get your task force out of my way? I can't do anything about it."

And Baldy would go back to Ted, "I'm changing course to the north."

Here we had to fuel and then go in and hit the Marshalls. We had to go past all these islands on the way in, so I knew we'd meet opposition.

I said to Lee, who had the battleships--they were leaving soon after that--"This is either going to be a picnic or a bad time."**

We hoped that they'd be back by 8:00 o'clock, our strike. They got back about 11:00. They had four parachutes in the air at one time. The Japs knew we were coming, and were ready to shoot us up.

Unfortunately, we had loaded with torpedoes. Had the big planes been able to have told us that there weren't any carriers there, we would have loaded bombs. But the only way to get a carrier is with a torpedo.

I'm sorry, I think that's the reason the operation wasn't a success. We loaded torpedoes, but we were doing what we thought was right.

---

*Rear Admiral Frederick C. Sherman, USN, Commander Task Group 50.4.
**Rear Admiral Willis A. Lee, Jr., USN, Commander Battleships Pacific. For operations in December 1943 he was designated Commander Task Group 50.8.

As I said, we had four parachutes in the air at once. We saved them all, the destroyers did. They all got out all right, thanks to the destroyers.

There were no carriers in Kwajalein, and I couldn't see the justification for a second strike with tired pilots, tired airplanes. And with no setup or opportunity for surprise or anything like that.

So we closed the operation. Of course, I was criticized for that.

Q: By whom?

Admiral Pownall: I think Towers and King thought I should have gone in again.*

To commit good airplanes and good pilots to nothing but old merchant ships at Kwajalein under adverse conditions didn't make sense to me.

Q: I'm sure that, being on the spot, you had better judgment than they did.

Admiral Pownall: I thought so, too. It kept me from an extra star.

---
*Vice Admiral John H. Towers, USN, Commander Air Force Pacific Fleet; Admiral Ernest J. King, USN, Commander in Chief U. S. Fleet.

Q: Did it really?

Mrs. Pownall: You don't know that it did, Dear.

Q: I'm interested. Do you think it did, really?

Admiral Pownall: Yes.

Q: They did not give you credit for using your own judgment. Had you been told to go in for a second strike?

Admiral Pownall: No. I used my own judgment.

One thing that contributed--when we fueled that night, the <u>Lexington</u> got a torpedo in her. I was critical of the cruiser that was supposed to protect her stern.

So we got up a message to send to this particular cruiser, "Why the heck didn't you open fire? Why didn't you protect the <u>Lexington</u>?" It turned out that the captain of that cruiser had died on the bridge. So I said, "We don't condemn men who've passed on." So the matter was closed.

I told Admiral Nimitz, I think, about it personally, but there's nothing in the files about it.

Q: Do you remember what his reaction to that was?

Admiral Pownall: I don't know. He had a lot on his mind.

Q: I wanted to refer to one thing here in the book, in your foreword, in which you're telling about one of the instances of the lifeguard. This relates really back to Mili.

Do you remember in your foreword where you said your carrier groups were pounding away at Mili and adjacent airdromes. Two of the planes couldn't make the carrier and one crash-landed alongside a submarine. Do you remember the incident that you've told about in your foreword here, of this book?

Admiral Pownall: No, I don't remember.

Q: Let me have you read it over again, and tell me the story in your own words.

Admiral Pownall: The people were hurt, the submarine crew was even hurt, and they had some of our people. This was our own submarine. And one of our own submarines could shoot this submarine. I couldn't go through the rigmarole of confidential messages; we had to put them in code and all that. My chief of staff and I resorted to something. We used profanity and hillbilly.

Pownall #2 - 150

Q: What did you say, do you remember?

Admiral Pownall: No, but Admiral Nimitz made me take it out of the signal book. He said it wasn't fit.

Q: He did, really? I wish you could remember what you said.

Admiral Pownall: The enemy, of course, was bastards and all that. I don't remember that all now. I used terrible language, but it worked.

We sent it right out on the air and they got the message. The submarine got through and nobody shot him, and the doctor looked out for the kids. As far as I know, they got well.

But it was a case where in an emergency you can use American profanity that even a Jap dictionary couldn't interpret. And it worked.

Q: That was a very good story, and I wanted to put it on the tape. I wouldn't think it would make any difference what you possibly said if you were saving the lives of your people.

Admiral Pownall: Apparently it worked.

Pownall #2 - 151

Q: I'm sure that endeared you to the people who worked for you, too.

Admiral Pownall: Nimitz said, "It's not for the record."

Q: I want to ask you what it feels like to be a commanding officer of a task force. How do you feel, what goes on in your mind, what are your thoughts?

Admiral Pownall: Do the job. I had a doctrine about carrier operations.

It all depends on what you're commanding. I wanted to use the element of surprise as much as I could. Carrier operations that are successful, you have to use all the breaks you can get.

You commit so many pilots and planes to do a certain job. You know you're going to have certain losses, but you want to cut that down as much as possible. So the old man has to have this in mind--the pilot should be well trained and in excellent physical condition. And the airplane should be the best the country can give him.

And you should use the element of surprise as much as possible, hit where they're not looking.

Q: What are your thoughts in the day? What do you think

about after you've sent out a strike?

Admiral Pownall: Thinking about getting them back. You have to carry out your mission and get them back. That's all. I don't have any fancy, great--I'm not a poet.

Q: You make it sound easy, and I'm sure it was far from that.

Admiral Pownall: Oh, no, it's tough.

I might say when I was flag officer and went on the Yorktown, the doctor on the Yorktown had said that the admiral's quarters on the bridge were not satisfactory for human habitation. So they had to give me a little air and a little water. That was on the Yorktown.

Then on the Lexington, Felix said, "I'm sorry, Admiral, but I'll have to fix up your emergency cabin so you can live in it."

They were not ready, I guess, for flag officers afloat. We had to live on the bridge, you know.

Then once I remember with Jock--when that kamikaze came over. I had gone to the bathroom, to be frank. When I came back, Jock showed me where a bullet from a kamikaze had gone right where I was standing. So that's one time when I was . . .

Q: You were better off in the head than on the bridge.

Admiral Pownall: And also Jerry Wiltse was on the <u>San Diego</u>, I think it was.*

The <u>Yorktown</u> was shooting away at this plane that crashed right alongside of us. It's been picturized quite a bit. Jerry said in a message, "We're not Japs." Some of the bullets fired at this kamikaze went over on his ship.

Q: I'm sure they were exciting demanding, frustrating, bad days, and good days, some, maybe.

Admiral Pownall: True.

I think the great thing was--like the submarines had-- adequate recreation between strikes, no matter how much oil it took.

There is a picture which might be of interest to you, at Roi-Namur. There are only two men in that picture that are alive today.

Q: Admiral Pownall is talking to me about a picture which I'm going to describe.

There are nine men in the picture--Admiral Spruance, Admiral Conolly, James Forrestal, Harry Schmidt (Marine), Holland Smith, Ben Moreell, the civil engineer, Carlson,

---

*Rear Admiral Lloyd Jerome Wiltse, USN, Commander Cruiser Division Two, embarked in the USS <u>San Diego</u> (CL-53).

and Admiral Pownall taken at Roi-Namur.*

Besides yourself, which is the only other one living?

Admiral Pownall: Ben Moreell.

Q: It's certainly an interesting picture, lots of wonderful men in that.

You've given me some stories and vignettes and episodes out of that part of your life that are interesting and reflect your character, I believe.

Admiral Pownall: War is hell.

Q: Yes, it must be. I always feel guilty in a way sitting back and feeling other people were doing it.

After that segment of your career, Admiral, shall we go on to the next one?

Admiral Pownall: That was Commander Air Force Pacific Fleet with headquarters in Honolulu.

Mrs. Pownall: Was that when you went with Spruance?

---

*Vice Admiral Raymond A. Spruance, USN; Rear Admiral Richard L. Conolly, USN; Undersecretary of the Navy James V. Forrestal; Major General Harry Schmidt, USMC; Major General Holland M. Smith, USMC; Rear Admiral Ben Moreell, CEC, USN; Lieutenant Colonel Evans F. Carlson, USMC.

Admiral Pownall: Yes, one time there. See, we learned this: a commander of carriers shouldn't ride a carrier, because of submarines. Submarines became very active then.

We had the Indianapolis for a while with Spruance.* But for me to be on a big ship and use radio--we couldn't use radio because we should keep silence. So I had this idea that I'd go with Spruance, who had command of the fleet. He was the fleet commander, and I was the air boy under him. So we went together. Then we could send from the Indianapolis to Pete Mitscher.** Mitscher was their man in the field. So whatever we had in our mind, we could give to Pete. I don't know a better man we could give it to.

That's the way it--the rest of the war was . . .

Q: Was that because of your recommendation, that they shouldn't be on a carrier?

Admiral Pownall: Yes, I think so. I certainly . . .

Mrs. Pownall: But, Jerry, Marc Mitscher was sitting back here in . . .

---

*The cruiser Indianapolis (CA-35) was Spruance's flagship in his role as Commander Fifth Fleet.
**Rear Admiral Marc A. Mitscher, USN, Commander Task Force 58.

Pownall #2 - 156

Admiral Pownall: Well, he'd come out there.

Mrs. Pownall: Not when you were out there.

Admiral Pownall: Well, I mean, he came over to live with me in Honolulu.

Mrs. Pownall: That was earlier, Jerry, because he came out and relieved you of that job.

Admiral Pownall: I'm sorry.

Mrs. Pownall: Well, that's true, dear. Isn't that right? It's in the book.

Admiral Pownall: Well, anyway, I'll tell you a good thing about Marc. When he relieved me--of course, we were classmates and good friends and had been.

Q: What job were you on when he relieved you?

Admiral Pownall: I was Commander Task Force 50.

Q: He relieved you in the task force.
   You're talking about this small segment, when you and Mitscher and Spruance were all there together. You went as

Pownall #2 - 157

Commander Air Force Pacific, and Mitscher then had your job, of which he had relieved you.

Mrs. Pownall: But he [Mitscher] came right out from Coronado there.

Admiral Pownall: I'll tell a story about Pete. When I was Commander Air Force Pacific, he was down the south there and he came up. Although Admiral Nimitz invited him over to the big house, but Pete felt more at home with an old classmate.

He came in a plane and I was there to meet him. Out of the stern of the airplane came Pete. Arleigh Burke was his chief of staff.* Then came a retinue of Japs, five or six of them.

I said, "Pete, who are they?"

"Oh," he said, "they're some prisoners." I thought maybe the intelligence were with them.

I said, "Well, damn it, they don't have anything around them. They could have taken over your airplane."

"Oh," he said, "they wouldn't do that."

There they were, about five or six Japs, in the plane with these two men. It was a big transport plane. It was typical of old Marc.

---
*Captain Arleigh A. Burke, USN.

Pownall #2 - 158

Q: They hadn't heard about the taking over of planes like we have now, or maybe they would have. They could have taken over that plane and taken it anyplace, couldn't they?

Admiral Pownall: Yes.

Q: I think that's an interesting development that you were responsible for--having the commanding officer of the task force or the task group not ride the carrier. I had noticed that they didn't, in reading the stories, and I wondered about it.

Admiral Pownall: You can see what sense it makes.

Q: It seems to me that all your ideas had sense.

Admiral Pownall: Thank you.

Q: I feel foolish saying that when you've done so much.

Admiral Pownall: We rode with Spruance; he was a wonderful man. We rode the <u>Indianapolis</u>, and then we rode the <u>New Jersey</u>. I had the captain's daylight quarters on the <u>New Jersey</u>, which is a wonderful ship. The Truk operation--we were there at Truk. This is interesting--a classmate of mine, Carl Moore, was Spruance's chief of staff.* I was

―――――――
*Captain Charles J. Moore, USN.

the air guy. Carl had the idea that we shouldn't hit Truk, for what we'd accomplish. We'd lose a lot of personnel, and what would we have? We'd have an island down there in the Pacific, which wasn't in the route for further operations to Japan.

He wrote a paper on it--Carl was a bright man and still is--to give up the Truk operation. He brought it to me, and I said, "I think it's fine."

He took it in to Nimitz. Admiral Nimitz read it, approved it, and sent it on to Washington. Admiral King approved it. And it was all done within 48 hours, I think.

Carl with his idea had started it, so they bypassed it. When we bypassed Truk, we hit it with air, but we didn't land troops. We blockaded Truk.

Q: Again, I know that we did bypass Truk, but the details only you know probably, or the men who were there.

Admiral Pownall: Then I also remember while we were out there at Truk with the New Jersey and the Iowa--we noticed these Jap cruisers over to one side. Spruance said, "Hey, we'd better get out of here." With that, a couple of torpedoes went across the Iowa's box; these blankety blanks saw us and let go to try out the range.

Q: Anyway, you got out without being hit.

Admiral Pownall: That's right, we did. Pete made a good strike on Truk first, and later on Saipan, while we were out there.

I think that's all I have in my head right now about the Pacific, until I became Commander Marianas.

Q: Your next step then was to do the training job that you had been advising before, and which were certainly well fitted for.

You were Chief of Naval Air Training Command at Pensacola and Intermediate Training Command. Then under you was also Corpus Christi. Is that correct?

Admiral Pownall: All the stations were.

Q: How many were there?

Admiral Pownall: Corpus Christi was the big one; it had intermediate training. Glenview at Chicago was primary and pre-flight. Operational was Jacksonville.

Here are the honor men [referring to a picture]. There are only three of us kicking out of five. On the left is Andy McFall; in the middle is Charlie Mason, then Pownall, and then O. B. Hardison, and Ezra Kendall. Kendall and Hardison are both dead.

Kendall had the enlisted men, the mechanics and so forth, at Chicago. Then Felix Stump relieved him.

Hardison had the elementary and preflight with headquarters at Glenview. Mason had the intermediate with headquarters at Corpus Christi. McFall was at Jacksonville.

My headquarters were at Pensacola, at the big house, A, Quarters A.

Q: Lots of historic men have occupied those quarters, haven't they?

Admiral Pownall: We even had a ghost.

Q: Who was the ghost? What was the story of the ghost?

Admiral Pownall: He had yellow fever, Commodore Woolsey.* He had Quarters A, and he moved up to the penthouse on the top floor, which is just one room. There he lived and died. It's supposed that his ghost still lives there.

Q: Did he go up there to be away from people so he wouldn't contaminate others?

---
*Commodore W. B. Woolsey, USN, was commandant of the Pensacola Navy Yard and the first occupant of Quarters A when it was completed in 1874. See "Pensacola Poltergeist," Naval History, Winter 1989, page 55.

Mrs. Pownall: No, he went up there to get away from it himself. He got it while he was up there. They had a dumb waiter that they put in to take food up to him. He was supposed to have dressed himself up in his dress uniform to die. And he had a short leg. That's what you hear--you hear him coming down the stairs.

Q: Did you really hear him?

Mrs. Pownall: Yes, I heard him.

Putty Read, when he was there, he was captain of the air station before the war.* He tore that place apart to try to find out what it was. But they never found out what it was.

Q: It's as good to have a ghost story as anything else.

Admiral Pownall: I'll tell a funny one about Hardison and Andy McFall. One's from North Carolina and one's from South Carolina. When we had a conference in Pensacola, they always stayed with us.

The story is--Commodore Woolsey was mad, coming down with a suitcase in his hand.

Mrs. Pownall: One of them, McFall or Hardison, said he saw this person.

---
*Captain Albert C. Read, USN.

Admiral Pownall: Hardison said, "It's getting too hot around here, I'm leaving."

Mrs. Pownall: The ghost said he didn't want to live with those queer people.

Q: Oh, the ghost was leaving because he didn't want to live with them. That's a good way to get rid of the ghost.

That was an enormous command and enormous responsibility. I'd like to have you tell me as much of it as you recall.

Admiral Pownall: That training command was something.

First of all, in the early days, we had started the cadet program. We'd take a college graduate and make a pilot out of him. Then we ran out of college graduates. Then the second year we ran out of that. We had to start a school of our own. We had Iowa State, North Carolina, St. Mary's. We took over the whole college of St. Mary's, near San Francisco.

We had our system inspected by educators. We had one, the president of the University of Michigan, come and look us over and see whether we were doing it right.

Pownall #2 - 164

Q: We are discussing the training command with headquarters in Pensacola. I know that there were many interesting experiences that you had that took place during this period, admiral.

Admiral Pownall: We had a carrier in the bay, so that when kids were hot we could qualify them on a carrier.

We started the survival course. A lad, if he knew how, could be an advanced Boy Scout and live off the land. I don't think we brought in snails. Everything else, we did.

Mrs. Pownall: You dropped the boys in out-of-the-way places, where they couldn't get to anything.

Admiral Pownall: There are things you can eat, even snakes. The fellow that saw those signs that you can live on 98 calories a day. He saw that and said it was wrong; you can't live on that.

We had a lot of visitors. I had good friends up in Washington, and they had the hard jobs. It was easy to be in training after being in Washington. Pete Mitscher and Roy Geiger flew down to get a little rest.* We were going out fishing and relax. I remember Pete went to sleep with a fish on his hook, which showed how tired those lads

---

*Major General Roy S. Geiger, USMC.

were. Then we went out to go again to Key Biscayne.

Pearson, the journalist, got ahold of it and wrote it all up in Washington.* That Admiral Mitscher, General Geiger, and Admiral Pownall were going fishing in a Navy's plane and were extravagant with government funds and gasoline. It ended up the story with, "But they didn't go."

Q: Unfortunately that was his stock in trade. That's how he sold his articles, by saying things that tended to be sensational.

Were you able to put into effect the things that you had believed to be good for training?

Admiral Pownall: Yes, we had the carrier in the Gulf of Mexico. And we had the survival program.

Mrs. Pownall: Didn't they have survival before you got there?

Admiral Pownall: No, not to my knowledge.

---
*Drew Pearson, a muckraking syndicated newspaper columnist.

Pownall #2 - 166

And I think our scholastic standard was a little higher with personnel. We succeeded in getting Comstock, for example, who was quite an educator. He was head of the school. There's a lot of work to educating boys to fly.

Mrs. Pownall: Didn't he come from Princeton, dear?

Admiral Pownall: I think it was Princeton.

Mrs. Pownall: He was a doctor or a professor with a degree or two.

Admiral Pownall: We also had medical research at Pensacola--the psychiatric and getting dizzy business. We ran it right there. It was under me administratively. Dr. Grossbeck was really the head of it.

Q: Whom did you relieve?

Admiral Pownall: Admiral George Dominic Murray. He's dead now.

Mrs. Pownall: He relieved Charles in the Pacific as Commander Air Force Pacific.

Admiral Pownall: I guess George wouldn't mind this. He

Pownall #2 - 167

was a devout Catholic, and when he was out in Guam, of course, Guam was 98% Catholic. I don't know, George and the bishop had a little . . .

Mrs. Pownall: I wouldn't go into that.

Q: They had a squabble?

Mrs. Pownall: Now, you don't know that they did or not.

Admiral Pownall: I don't know that they did--only they replaced George with a Quaker.

Mrs. Pownall: I don't think that had anything to do with it.

Admiral Pownall: All right. We'll leave that out. It's in there, though.

Mrs. Pownall: Is there anything more about Pensacola?

Q: I'm sure you did a lot of traveling, didn't you?

Mrs. Pownall: Yes, all over the country, inspecting all those places.

Admiral Pownall: The man that ran St. Mary's was a reserve, an ex-aviator. He was about six feet one. He had been a football player at Annapolis. They all stood up before a megaphone and said wonderful things about St. Mary's. When it came my turn, they had to bring the megaphone down to my height. I said, "I'm sorry, I didn't go to St. Mary's."

I think that's about all on the training command.

Q: I'm looking at a beautiful sterling silver punch bowl. It was "Presented to Rear Admiral and Mrs. Charles A. Pownall by the Chamber of Commerce in Pensacola in grateful appreciation, 19 December 1945."

I don't want to leave this command, without mentioning your Legion of Merit that you were awarded for exceptionally meritorious conduct from September 9, 1944, to August 31, 1945. It says:

"Displaying the highest order of leadership, initiative, foresight, sound planning, and administrative ability, he directed the vast and complicated training organization under his command in delivering to the fleet approximately 14,000 trained naval aviators and 24,000 trained combat air crewmen who, by their performance in combat against the enemy in all theaters of the war against the Axis, have passed on to the service of the Navy and the nation the results of his inspired leadership and devotion to duty."

Again, I do note that your planning ability is mentioned.

Admiral Pownall: In that job you had to plan.

Q: I'm sure. I don't feel as though maybe you've given me all of the important . . .

Mrs. Pownall: One time a father came down and accepted the Congressional Medal of Honor posthumously for his son. He had thrown his body over a hand grenade to save four of his companions. That was while we were down there.

Q: Why was it awarded there? Had it happened there?

Admiral Pownall: He lived there, right near Pensacola. He was an aviator, and had been killed out in the Pacific.

Q: Let's go on to this duty which I'm sure would be a highlight, I would think--your duty in the Marianas and Guam. Since I know very little about that--I know something of the history of Guam, I'd like for you to start from the beginning and tell me everything you can remember about it. This, I think, was strictly yours. Nobody else was there at that time. It could only be you and your recollection that makes the history for the Institute.

Admiral Pownall: I was ordered first as Commander Marianas. That's the Carolines, Palau, and the Gilberts--a lot of ocean, a lot of islands.

I made it a rule to go every place I could by air. So I did a lot of flying while I was there. The small islands that we couldn't get to by airplane, Admiral Wright, my deputy, made with a doctor and a dentist.* So we covered the islands pretty well.

I was impressed, for example, with the natives on Ulithi. That's nothing but a bunch of small islands south of Guam. We, of course, used a lot of belly tanks in the planes. The one thing they wanted was water. Water was very scarce, because the only fresh water they had they got off the roofs. Here we had a whole warehouse full of these. The war was over, and they didn't touch a one of them. So I really exceeded my authority, but I gave them the warehouse full of belly tanks so that they could have water tanks on their roofs.

One other thing that impressed me was when we went in there the Marines had moved out. The Marines moved out in a hurry and they left their tools, like wrenches, right on the bench. You'd think that a native would pick up the wrench, but not one of them had been touched. Nobody stole

---
*Rear Admiral Carleton H. Wright, USN, Deputy High Commissioner of the Pacific Trust Territories.

anything. That's just a plain G-string native, at Ulithi.

Then Yap--that was an interesting island with all the heavy money. They were fine people, too. We could land on Yap.

Palau had Koror. The Palau Islands were the Japanese Pearl Harbor, in a sense. They had shipyards at Palau, not at Truk but at Palau. We brought back a copper fish from there.

Mrs. Pownall: It was on the high altar of the temple at Koror, way up on the mountainside. It's a carp, their sacred fish.

Admiral Pownall: Koror is the capital of Palau Islands in the Western Pacific.

The Admiralty Islands came under us. We had to send doctors down there. That was under the British.

General MacArthur came into the Philippines through the south approach.* One thing that was interesting--they had a few fights down there.** Swift had the First Cavalry, United States Army. He had lost some men.

At dinner that night, he asked me if I had any grass seed. I said, "I don't know, but I think I can scare up some grass seed."

---
*General Douglas MacArthur, USA.
**Major General Innis P. Swift, USA, Commanding General, First Cavalry Division.

He said, "Because I have two dozen Kentucky boys, and I have to bury them. I don't want to put sand over them; I want to put topsoil. I can get the topsoil, but I can't get the grass seed."

So when I got back to Honolulu (this is before), I said to Jimmy Boundy, the supply officer, "I want 150 pounds of grass seed.* I don't care where you get it, but get it." So he got it and I sent it to Swift. One day I asked Jimmy where he got it. I said, "Jim, where did you get the grass seed?"

He said, "Oh, I picked it up at Fort Shafter."

Q: That was before you went out as governor of Marianas?

Admiral Pownall: Yes.

Q: What was it like when you went there? How did the natives feel toward you? Was there destruction on the islands? Where did you live when you first went to be governor?

Admiral Pownall: On Guam, with headquarters there.

Q: That's what I wondered, because it reads that you assumed duty as Commander Marianas. That was in February.

---
*Commander James W. Boundy, SC, USN.

Pownall #2 - 173

Then in May, "With the approval of the President, the Secretary of the Navy directed that you reestablish the naval government at Guam." And thereafter served as naval Governor of Guam--as though there were two.

Admiral Pownall: The two were combined; I had two staffs. I had the island organization, everything right on the island, everything on Guam. My headquarters was Admiral Nimitz's old office.

Mrs. Pownall: The headquarters was up 100 feet in the air. And his governor's office was down in Agana, in a hollow as hot as hell almost. It was terrific. He spent one half of the day down there, and one half as Commander Marianas.

Q: Would you clarify that?

Admiral Pownall: I had part of the day as Commander Marianas in the upper quarters, which was Admiral Nimitz's old headquarters. Then in the afternoon generally, I'd go down to Agana and answer my mail down there as governor of Guam. We used the old hospital as the governor's headquarters.

Mrs. Pownall: All that had been destroyed. The old palace

was destroyed; the cathedral was destroyed.

Q: Tell me what it was like when you went there.

Admiral Pownall: It was devastated. It was in ruins from the war. We took over the whole island.

Eventually we tried to pay it back to the native people. We had land reallocation. We had three or four officers. We paid them back $11 million eventually.

Mrs. Pownall: They destroyed trees, they destroyed houses. Some of those houses were well-built and big houses.

Q: You were on Guam?

Mrs. Pownall: Yes, I went right out. He went out in February and I went out in May. I wasn't there when it was bombed, but I saw the destruction. It was terrific.

Admiral Pownall: We had land title claims department with a four-stripe captain of supply as head of it. We made surveys and tried to do it right.

We had one rule, while we were getting back to battery--that the business of the islands was restricted to the Guamanians for the time being. Towers didn't like it, but I was working under Spruance and MacArthur.

One thing about MacArthur--to explain the command relations. The general thought it best if he was the senior and commanded the whole Pacific, just like Sharp has.* Somehow, the Joint Chiefs couldn't see that. They thought it was too much power in one man. General MacArthur didn't stand too well in some circles, but I liked him. So they compromised by turning the Mariana Islands over to General MacArthur's command administratively. I was Commander Marianas, so I came under him for administrative things.

Then I got orders from Admiral Nimitz to go back to Tokyo to talk to General MacArthur, because I had the idea to give my command over to an Air Force man. Admiral Nimitz wanted to discourage that, because it was really a Navy job with all the ships. It had been for years. I wanted to try to get up to the Bonins. You had to go through the Bonins to get to Tokyo, Chi Chi Jima, which is another story. I had a hard time making it. We froze up our engines. Finally had to practically disobey flight regulations, but we got in.

MacArthur had his chief of staff to do this conference. Then he came in. The upshot of it was that not only did the general agree to let the Navy keep the Marianas and Guam, but he gave unified command, as far as the Air Force and Army was concerned, to the Navy. And I was the Navy

---
*Admiral U. S. Grant Sharp, USN, was Commander in Chief Pacific from 1964 to 1968.

man there.

Q: So you must have accomplished that mission satisfactorily, too.

Admiral Pownall: Yes.

Mrs. Pownall: He had Army, Navy, and Air Force all on that island under him. So it was always going to be a little struggle, unless they made somebody at the top.

Admiral Pownall: We had two big Air Force fields up in the north of the island. We had Agana in the center. And Orote in the Peninsula. So there were four airports on Guam--pretty good size, too.

Our orders were not only to run Guam and the Marianas, but to support forces to the westward, at Banchana. We had Marines, of course, in China.

Every now and then, I'd have to go around the circuit, to see what was going on. This one time the Chief of Naval Operations said, "You fly your flag on the Randall. And Mrs. Pownall may accompany you, if she so desires."

Mrs. Pownall: So I did desire.

Admiral Pownall: First we stopped at Manila. Then we went to the Bonins.

Mrs. Pownall: That was the first time an American admiral had been on those islands since Perry stopped there.

I think there were some American women there. After the war, I was the first one.

We had an American governor on that island, and an English governor on that island at one time.

Admiral Pownall: The Japs used them as coaling stations. They were a little tricky for aircraft, but they were might good as coaling stations and a submarine base. And that's what the Japs did.

Mrs. Pownall: But there hadn't been any other people out there.

One thing--the President decided to reestablish the government laws of Guam. They had laws before the war. They had military law before this, which was very different from civil law. All of a sudden, when I was made governor, we had civil laws. It was very different. We had to go back to civil laws.

Q: Did you have to do a lot of studying to know what the civil laws were?

Pownall #2 - 178

Admiral Pownall: No, I had good lawyers. They kept me out of trouble. I had to use common sense and I said, "If that doesn't work, you'll have to keep me out of jail."

Mrs. Pownall: We had this one friend who said, "That's why I'm here, to keep him out of jail."

Q: How large a staff did you have, admiral?

Admiral Pownall: In the Marianas it was as big as the commander-in-chief's. You can see why, with land claims and medical jobs.

Mrs. Pownall: Some of these tremendous companies came out there to build up the island again. There were 24,000 Guamanians and 200,000 civilians and soldiers and military out there when we were there.

Admiral Pownall: We had two billion worth of excess material.

Q: Was that your job, to dispose of it properly?

Admiral Pownall: Yes. We wanted to get it back to the United States, but the people back in the United States didn't want it.

So the State Department, with Tom McCabe, figured it out that we owed Nationalist China some debts for fields that we'd used.* The decision of the State Department was to use the material to pay it back.

So the Chinese sent over at least a battalion, with General Ting commanding, to assemble this excess material and load it aboard ship and take it back to China.

Q: I never heard that before.

Admiral Pownall: We gave it to them. Some of the stuff they put back in Shanghai, I guess it's still there. The Chinese can do wonders with secondhand material, but some of this stuff they couldn't. I think one was dental chairs.

Mrs. Pownall: You should have seen the warehouses just stacked with stuff, everything from fountain pens to everything you can imagine.

Q: Brought in from all over the Pacific and stored there in warehouses?

Admiral Pownall: Yes. I thought if I got through this job

---
*Thomas B. McCabe, Foreign Liquidation Commissioner and Special Assistant to the Secretary of State.

without getting court-martialed, I'd be happy--two billion dollars worth of material.

Mrs. Pownall: They did have quite a little bit--as you always do have when you get stuff that you can't watch every bit of it--they had quite a little bit of trouble with people taking it. Not natives, but people could get to it.

Admiral Pownall: Admiral Nimitz wouldn't let dependents come out there, until after I went out and reported whether I could handle dependents. I went out and the decision was, "Yes, after he says that the quarters are satisfactory for his family." He had to sign a statement that the quarters were satisfactory.

I knew the quarters were. We were using excess material to put in wiring, toilets, and that sort of thing. He who wanted his wife and baby to come out there would have to help reconstruct the quonset and make it habitable.

Mrs. Pownall: We had awfully nice quarters out there. And Charles' staff did. Around the hospital they had some. But outside of that, there wasn't much of anything. The Marine Corps had some.

Then the rest of those people that came out, the

husband had to make shift some kind of place that he could bring his wife before she could come out. They used a great many quonsets. I wish you could have seen how beautiful some of them were, the things those men did to those things. They'd put two or three big quonsets together, and they'd have a patio. My daughter lived in one after she was married out there.

Admiral Pownall: One thing, too--laws of Guam prohibited gambling, except cockfights. My sweetie doesn't gamble, except for slot machines out there and bridge. Here I am Commander Marianas. We'd go around to the Marines . . .

Mrs. Pownall: Charles never had it up where he was, he wouldn't have any slot machines up in his part.

Admiral Pownall: But I didn't want to interfere with the Marines. They raised money for the welfare fund and all that, so I didn't insist. They had it for athletic gear and all that, so I wasn't going to get hard-boiled. The Marine Corps knew the situation. They had a slot machine room, and they took Mary down to the slot machine room.

Mrs. Pownall: They'd always lock it up when Charles came down for parties. But they'd always take me out and let me play the slot machines.

Q: What was the island where the man knew the "Star-Spangled Banner?"

Admiral Pownall: Kusae.

I flew in there in a patrol plane and went ashore. He said he'd like to pay his respects. He said he'd served under the Germans and the Spanish and the Japs, and now under the United States Government. He was the chief of the island.

The Seventh-day Adventists and the Baptists, who were their missionaries, did a wonderful lot of good for those people and for the United States. Most of them had a very high sense of patriotism, as evidenced by this old fellow getting up and singing the "Star-Spangled Banner." Every school you went to, you heard the "Star-Spangled Banner" all right. Kusae, and Ponape were two cases where it was so much in evidence.

Mrs. Pownall: In Guam, too, those people were so patriotic. Down at the lower end of the island, where the big farms are, the Japanese went down there. They wouldn't give one bit of food to those Japanese. They took those farmers out and put them over a ditch and chopped their heads off, even the priest that was at the church down there. Isn't that terrible.

Admiral Pownall: It would have been easy for the Guamanians to play along with them.

I said, when I went over to relieve Murray, "How many sons of bitches have you on the island?" (Meaning those that weren't loyal.)

He said, "One, and he's a native-born Jap."

I said, "Frankly I can't believe that. After all, it would have been easier for them to play along with the conquering Japs."

He said, "That's all I could find."

So I had sort of a board of Marines, and we went into a real investigation of how many of those that were disloyal, and we couldn't find more than this one. And he was a native-born Jap. I got him off the island. I asked General MacArthur if he could take him up there in Tokyo and he did. We got him off the island, because I don't think he'd have lived very long.

Q: Were there any Japanese holed up on the island?

Admiral Pownall: First of all, we were losing Marines, because they went out to search out the Japs.

What happened was that there was no official surrender on the island. So it was every Jap for himself, so to speak, or in groups, instead of a whole army surrendering and going off under command. That meant that there would be a lot of stragglers, a lot of people hiding out.

The thing that was wrong was they were killing our young Marines. Because I was boss, I turned it around the other way. We armed the farmers and let them come to us, instead of we going out to them. So that changed the score quite a bit of our fatalities.

Down at Palau we had a lot of Japs in caves. We couldn't get them out, and we didn't want to blow them out or kill them just that way. So we sent a Jap prisoner, a general, down to tell them that the war was over and that it would be all right for them to go home. They were afraid their own people would disown them, but we finally got them out. It was touch and go there for a while, whether we'd have to blow them out.

People from down in the middle of the island of Guam used to go up to the north and go swimming, and there we had Japs hiding out up there. We finally captured a Jap that needed a haircut.

Mrs. Pownall: Then you thought they were all gone, but they weren't, because they found some later. Even after we came home, they found them.

When we were out there, our daughter went with a party up there to the northern part. They were going to go in some of the caves. We had General Craig with us there for lunch on the day she was going out on this picnic up in the northern part of the island.*

He had a Marine detachment up in the northern part and he told her, "You be careful. Don't go in those caves, unless you have with you two or three men that are armed, because you never can tell when you're going to run into a Jap." So they went up there.

They had Marine stations at that time. This was quite a while after they thought they had them pretty well cleared out. They went through the sentry box, on down onto the beach, stayed down there and had lunch and so forth.

When they came back, the whole Marine sentry's box had been blown up. The boy was all right; he had gotten away all right. It was Japs from one of those caves. Fortunately, they didn't try to go in those caves that afternoon, after what General Craig told them.

She didn't even come out there until '47. We went out in '46. We had been there that long, and there were that many Japanese.

When I first went out there, if I went into any other part of the island than right around where we were, our Marine driver always had a tommy gun right alongside him, on the driver's seat. They even did that when we drove around at night, going to different clubs and so forth on

---
*Brigadier General Edward A. Craig, USMC.

the island. There was a great deal of interchange of parties and so forth, because that's about all they had to do out there, except swim and so forth. They had some beautiful parties. It's beautiful country, of course. When we traveled through that, we always had to take a gun.

Q: What was the implication of his remark--that you found a Jap that needed a haircut?

Mrs. Pownall: It was only one person; there was nobody to cut his hair. So when they found this one with long hair, they thought they didn't have any other ones.

Q: They figured that was the last one, but it wasn't?

Mrs. Pownall: It wasn't, far from it.

Way up there at the north, they had a special kind of bat and they eat them. They take the fur, or whatever it is, off of them, and it's just exactly like the white meat of chicken. I've eaten it. I hated it.

This is something that was given to both of us. They have very fine silversmiths out there.

Q: I'm holding a cylinder. Is there a scroll inside?

Mrs. Pownall: Yes. The bishop's seal is on one end, and

the seal of Guam is on the other. It's the Catholic Church. A Guamanian silversmith made that.

Q: It's just beautiful. It has lots of open work and it says, "To his Excellency, Rear Admiral C. A. Pownall, Governor of Guam. United Societies Catholic Church of Guam, August 21st, 1948."

Mrs. Pownall: That was farewell.

Q: On this scroll is a resolution saying that:

"Whereas his Excellency, Rear Admiral Charles A. Pownall, United States Navy, Governor of Guam, and Mrs. Pownall have always shown themselves deeply interested in the work and welfare of the Parish Societies of the Catholic Church of Guam, and whereas they have manifested that interest repeatedly by participating in our rallies, congresses, and other meetings of these societies, and whereas the Governor and first lady of Guam will soon be departing from our shores after the years of self-sacrificing labor among our people, now therefore be it resolved that the United Catholic Societies of Guam, as represented by the Bishop of Guam and the chosen representative of each of the Parish Societies, signed and delivered to the Governor and first lady a copy of this resolution, together with a silver case in which it may be preserved, as a souvenir of the affection in which they will ever be held by the members of our organization."

It's signed by the Bishop, the president of the Christian Mothers Societies and the president of the Sodality of Mary, Guam, dated on the 21st day of August, 1948.

It's a beautiful memory, isn't it?

Mrs. Pownall: Yes.

The Guam Congress, and all the Guamanian people, sent back enough money to have a portrait painted of the admiral and hung in the Guam Congress.

Q: You have the picture of the portrait, above the members of the Congress. That was in 1950, after it became a territory.

Mrs. Pownall: The admiral had a great deal to do with that Congress being built. He had all the planning done for it.

Q: Did you do the planning for Guam to become a territory under the act?

Admiral Pownall: No, it was already--one thing was we wanted to be sure that they were ready for self-government. They had a committee come out--Ernest Hopkins of Dartmouth and Mills Rice of the University of California--three men who came out to look us over. They recommended that it stay under the Navy just as it was.

The Department of Interior wanted it. They wanted to hire more people. So to make a long story short, it was turned over to the Department of Interior.

Q: Under the Organic Act of Guam of 1950 as amended.

Mrs. Pownall: They sent the money back here, and the admiral sat for the portrait. Then it was framed. They sent $1,500 back here to have his portrait painted and framed and sent out.

Q: Very touching, isn't it?

Admiral Pownall: Notice all the Guam Congress have neckties, they're in uniform.

Q: That is their uniform? They're in uniform if they have a necktie?

Admiral Pownall: Before that they just came any way. They were sort of hippy, but I wouldn't let them be hippy.

They walked out on me one time. And that was very serious, because the Guam Congress represented the whole island. I said, "If you're not back in 24 hours, we'll consider the seat vacant." They were back. They were striking. You had to teach them, you had to lead them around a little bit.

Admiral Pownall: When he was about to retire, they put in a petition that he stay on as their governor after he retired. Of course, by that time, they had made up their minds it was going to go under civilians.

Q: You told me also during that period there was the episode of moving the bodies of the Americans who had died in the Pacific.

Admiral Pownall: We had them on Guam and all through the islands, Saipan.

I reported that the native people almost treated it as their responsibility to look after American dead in the cemeteries. They spent very little money on it; it was just natural.

So we had to rip them up and put them in sacks. It was terrible.

Q: I think you said that Saltonstall came out. Tell me that episode.

Admiral Pownall: Yes. He was a senator and he flew out with the Air Force and stayed with us.* He had a son who was killed. I took him down to see his son's grave in a cemetery in Agana. He said that he was the one that thought it ought to be brought back to Honolulu; the boy's mother said no. He agreed that the mother was right and he was wrong, when he saw it.

Q: When he saw the circumstances.

Mrs. Pownall: When he saw the way they were treated, the way they looked out for them.

Admiral Pownall: I went to Guadalcanal to see some other lad's. I forgot who it was who had a boy buried on Guadalcanal. But Guadalcanal had quite a cemetery.

Q: It must have been, if they buried everybody there that died there, and on most of all of the islands.

Admiral Pownall: I think it was wrong to move them. After all, you didn't know what you were moving.

Q: I wanted you to tell me something of the government of

_____
*Leverett Saltonstall, a Republican, was governor of Massachusetts, 1938-44, and a U. S. senator from that state, 1944-67.

Pownall #2 - 192

Guam, and what your actual duties were in carrying it out.

Admiral Pownall: It was a territorial government, in which the governor had his assembly. They had a senate and a house, elected, and a commissioner. Every so often, there'd be a town and there would be a commissioner. He was elected and paid by the governor. He wasn't an elected officer, but we made sure we had good commissioners.

Q: You appointed him?

Admiral Pownall: Yes, on the recommendation of a good many Guamanians.

Of course, it was new to them. They had had a government before. Jimmy Alexander was one of the best, and he was before the war.*

But to hold them down to raise money themselves and to actually produce was--they said, "Pownall, you made a mistake. You should have gone back and asked for about four or five million. Instead of that you didn't ask for any."

I said, "No, I want the Guamanians to start learning how to raise a little money themselves." And eventually they did.

But that's my contribution, I think, to get the

---
*Captain George A. Alexander, USN, governor of Guam from June 1933 to March 1936.

Guamanians to see the joy of self-respect. They certainly came back through it.

Q: Did you feel that you had accomplished something at that time?

Admiral Pownall: I think I did. At least [inaudible] appreciated it. I was supposed to be tough.

Q: Were you, did you consider yourself so?

Admiral Pownall: No. I had to do what was right. I had to represent the government of the United States, as well as the people of Guam.

Q: This was a completely new type of duty for you.

Admiral Pownall: Yes, true, it was.
 But when you command a ship, after all, you have to know the difference between right and wrong when administering your ship.

Q: A governor is a little different than a commanding officer, isn't it? Did you take the advice of these people who were in the assembly?

Admiral Pownall: Yes, I tried to. We had our rights, so to speak, and they could override my veto and go to the President of the United States. I don't believe there ever was a time when we didn't settle our own affairs.

Q: Did you have to veto many bills?

Admiral Pownall: No, not very many. We tried to explain it to them beforehand, and tried to get the sense of reasoning in their heads, and not to let it come to the vote until it had been thoroughly exhausted. Money was the main thing.

Q: What was the language, what were they speaking?

Admiral Pownall: Talagi, it's a Malay dialect.

Q: How did you make communication with them?

Admiral Pownall: They spoke English also. Some couldn't but most of them could. In the congress it was all in English.

Q: What about the schools?

Admiral Pownall: The schools were in English.

Q: How about establishing, there weren't any schools there when you went there, were there?

Admiral Pownall: Yes, there were some. We started a high school.

Mrs. Pownall: Every one of the provinces had schools.
That's one thing that I did when we were out there--at Christmas time we had real Christmas trees brought out. In every one of those schools in each one of those provinces, we had a Christmas tree and a real celebration. The Red Cross sent me out an awful lot of stuff. We went over with truckloads of stuff to get enough gifts for each one of those children.

Q: This was just in Guam, not all the Marianas.

Mrs. Pownall: Oh, yes, just in Guam. You'd be surprised what there was to do there.

Q: You couldn't possibly have done it throughout all the islands.

Admiral Pownall: Remember Colonel McCormick of the Chicago

Tribune? He came out, he and his wife. He was on his way to China.

I said, "Sir, down there is the island where Magellan came in."* I was taking him around the islands.

Mrs. Pownall: This is a map that was made by the engineers out there as a gift when we left. Here is the old Spanish galleon that brought him in. It's on its way into that place where he's supposed to have landed.

You know the story of when we took over the island in the Spanish-American war, don't you?

Q: I know we took it over. I don't know what the story is.

Mrs. Pownall: The story is that they came in there and fired into the place to show that they were coming in to capture it. The Spanish governor came out in a little boat and apologized. They said they didn't have any kind of powder, so they couldn't return the salute. They were firing on them to take it over.

Admiral Pownall: McCormick said he'd like to get some rocks from down at Merizo. So I had the Marine orderly

---

*Ferdinand Magellan was a Portuguese explorer who led an expedition that circumnavigated the earth in the 16th century.

load up a couple of rocks. I said, "I can't fly them back; they're too heavy."

He said, "We want the Tribune Tower to honor Magellan. It's been a long time since he was around." So he eventually got the rocks back to Chicago and they're now in the tower there, of the Chicago Tribune in honor of Magellan.

Q: Did you really get him rocks from down there, or did you just pick some out of the back yard?

Admiral Pownall: Yes, I think McCormick went himself.

Mrs. Pownall: That's what he had them publish the first Sunday after he got back, in the Tribune. That's the original.

Q: This is interesting. Let me see if I can describe it. It's a cartoon, it's almost a two-decker cartoon.

There's a picture at the top with the caption, "Watchdog of the Pacific." There's three people, prehistoric looking almost. One says, "Big dipper, look grandpa, drong." and they're looking at the sky. The bottom shows two Russians, one in uniform and the other in a smock. The Russian in uniform has a question mark over his head. The one in the smock says, "Look, Uncle Joe, bow

bow." Then the wording says, "Primitive people of ancient times imagined they could see things in the sky. I wonder if the primitive people of today can see anything in the water."

The point is that the islands in the Pacific--Hawaii he's made the tail and a dotted line to Midway, the back of a dog, down to Wake, over to Iwo Jima and down to Okinawa. Then down to Guam is the mouth of the dog. Saipan, Kwajalein, and Truk are the mouth. The feet are the South Pacific Islands. Then up under the stomach are the Marshall Islands and Johnston Island.

It's very clever. The top one is the dipper. And the bottom one is the dog made of the islands, and it says U. S. airfields and bases. The whole thing is "Watchdog of the Pacific." And he dedicates it to Admiral Charles Pownall from the Chicago Tribune, December 13, 1947, "With best wishes, Barry Orr." That took three columns of the Saturday four colors in the Tribune. That's marvelous, isn't it?

Admiral Pownall: The Japs had pretty well ruined the livestock and chickens; there wasn't any. So we brought in both cattle and chickens. The Guam farmers would put up the money--that was one thing I did for these fellows--to pay for the cattle before the cattle ships arrived. In other words, they didn't borrow. Of course they used

American Navy ships to haul the cattle and chickens in, but we didn't have to finance very much. We did a little, but most of it came from them themselves.

Q: And where did they get any money, from their farming?

Admiral Pownall: After we paid them back those millions from their claims, and a good conscientious farmer always had a little in his sock someplace.

Mrs. Pownall: They had very good farm stores, because we used to buy from them. We had a wonderful garden of our own.

Q: Had there been any attempt to rehabilitate Guam during the time that Admiral Nimitz had his headquarters out there?

Admiral Pownall: No, we were fighting the war. We used all the land for military purposes, airports. We had a big ammunition depot on Guam; I don't know how many acres it took. There were rehabilitation hospitals. There wasn't much left, when we got through with it. We were pretty busy; we didn't have time for nice things.

Q: When you came, then it was under you that the first

attempt at rehabilitation--the properties and the cities and the road.

Admiral Pownall: Yes, and we would not let the businessmen from New York or Honolulu come in there. Of course, they had more technique. We wanted the Guamanians, the grocery man, the dry goods store, and so forth, to have a chance to get going again.

So I was very unpopular with a lot of people, because I wouldn't let them come and sell their goods and exploit people. And we kept it that way for a couple of years.

Mrs. Pownall: When the civilians came in, they changed all of that. For all the time that Charles was there, he had them entirely on their own.

Admiral Pownall: I have to thank Admiral Nimitz and Spruance.

Mrs. Pownall: They backed you on that.

Admiral Pownall: There were those that thought it was wrong, that it should have been the American way to get it going and to use American industry to get it going. But I wanted to use Guamanian industry to get Guamanians going.

Q: I would certainly think that's the way. Were there many Guamanians away that came back as soon as the war was over?

Admiral Pownall: Some served in the armed forces. Some of them worked for the supply department. No, we didn't have very many that came back.

Q: Mostly they were the people that stayed there and remained during the war. I don't know how they lived under the Japanese.

Mrs. Pownall: They were perfectly wonderful. They raised their own food and took care of each other. They had a terribly bad time.

Q: It must have been impossible. I had thought maybe they were all exterminated, and that they came back after the war.

Admiral Pownall: Only those that were down there that were beheaded.

We had a very trying case; we had a prostitute in jail. What are you going to do with a prostitute?

There was a Catholic Priest, Father Alvin, who was a very fine shortstop on the Detroit Tigers team before he went into the priesthood.

The Bishop called me up one day and said, "Father Alvin would like to see you, governor."

I said, "All right, I'll be right there."

He said, "I think I can solve this situation you're in, this problem you have. If you release her in the morning, I'll have her married by sundown."

So that's the way it ended. That was Father Alvin; he's dead now.


Q: That was like the decisions of Solomon.

Did you institute medical programs throughout the islands while you were there?


Admiral Pownall: I had some good doctors. You can give them the credit for it.

One case was when a truck in the Admiralties went over a cliff. We got the message, but we couldn't send them that day because they couldn't land on there at night. The next morning we sent an operating team--nurses, surgeons, and all--on one big plane. They did about eight or nine skull operations and they had a wonderful score of recoveries. We got a letter of appreciation from the governor of the Philippines.

Then we got rid of yaws, with penicillin, throughout the Marianas and Guam. The fellow that discovered penicillin certainly helped out with yaws.

Q: You told me that you had a bad fall when you were out there.

Admiral Pownall: We had heard that the water was bad on Babelthuap, and we had to find out about it. So I went down with the staff and landed in a place where you could land. We went up through the schoolhouse area, and went across where the water comes in; this bridge is over a creek. The bridge went down, and I went down with it. On top of me came some pretty heavy boys. One was on me, and I'm not very big.

Mrs. Pownall: One of your aides.

Admiral Pownall: Yes. I got out of the place and they helped me up. Out of this shack came this native with a satchel with a carton of things. It was marked, "U. S. Medical Corps." He made the statement, "If you'd been a Jap, I wouldn't be here very long."

Of course, I realized then it was up to me to get my face lifted all right, so I sent him $50.00 for the school children's book fund. Then I thought I ought to do something else. We got a pregnant pig and sent it down by airplane. She was named Josephine. She produced a few hours after they got her out of the airplane.

Q: Did you tell me he had sent you $50.00?

Admiral Pownall: Yes, for my damages.

Q: And you returned it to him to be part of the children's book fund. Then came the pig.

Admiral Pownall: I had face, pig gave me face. I think he wanted a little face, too. They were run over a good bit by the Japs.

Finally, he sent me these two shells. The Navy was very kind to include them in our household goods.

Q: Those big, giant clam shells. So he was the last gift giver.

I'm sure that was an interesting tour.

Did you enjoy being first lady?

Mrs. Pownall: I loved it. I just loved being out there. We had the best time out there. It was intensely interesting.

There was that first around-the-world flight on Pan American, with all those newspaper people on it. That's another story. They came out there, and Charles had it all set up for them. Our houses all had four bathrooms, the whole staff, each one of them. He thought that the very first thing they'd want would be a bath after getting off the plane in all that heat. No, they wanted a good drink.

They got in there about 5:00 or 6:00 o'clock in the morning. They were to spend the whole day out there, all over the island.

Then they came to our house after they had had their drink. Everybody had divided up and taken their baths; there were about 56 of them. Then they came and had breakfast. We had everything--all the fruit juices, fruit, scrambled eggs, sausage, coffee, and tea. I had a wonderful cook.

We had four servants in the house all the time. When we had anything like this, we got more. They thoroughly enjoyed it. That's one incident.

Then they came back--we were all so tired, we'd been up since very early with all these people coming in. They had been very much delayed, because there was something wrong with their plane. They didn't get off until very late in the afternoon. The next thing we knew, they were all back. Something had happened to the air-conditioning, but they did get off that night.

Admiral Pownall: There were a lot of interesting people.

Trippe was one of them, the Pan American president.*

Q: You told me that Marquand, the author, visited you there.**

Admiral Pownall: Yes, he came out. He was with Louis Denfeld.*** Louis Denfeld was going out to China for something. And he invited Marquand to go along. So that's the way he happened to be on that trip.

When the first passenger flight came out from Pan American, the little stewardess came up and presented me with the most beautiful orchid corsage. We have a picture of that somewhere. We were 1,000 feet up in the air, and we were standing so you could look right straight over the Pacific when she presented it. It's such a beautiful view of the ocean.

Q: I'm going to put this on the tape, so it will remind you when you read it. Those pictures that you have down in the cellar in your material, please try to locate them and let the Institute have them. They'd be most appreciative.

Were things done very formally as governor and first lady?

---
*Juan Trippe.
**John Marquand.
***Admiral Louis E. Denfeld, USN, was Commander in Chief Pacific Fleet during most of 1947.

Mrs. Pownall: Some of them were. We really had beautiful dinners; there's no doubt about that. Everybody came in dinner clothes. The men didn't, because they didn't have any dress clothes out there at all. Until the end, they didn't even wear whites; they just wore khaki. But my husband insisted that they had to wear a necktie. That's about the only thing that they did.

Admiral Pownall: They had to wear a shirt with a necktie.

Q: They didn't have to wear jackets?

Admiral Pownall: No open chests. I didn't think that was very good.

Mrs. Pownall: The Army, clear up to the very end to the time we left, would come up to our house with neckties on. But when they entertained us, they never wore neckties. Of course, it was much hotter where they were down on the level. We were way up in the air, so we were cooler up there.

We had a big tremendous lanai that we did most of our entertaining on. We had a great big dining room and a big living room. When we were giving a big party, we could take care of a lot of people.

Pownall #2 - 208

Q: These are the quarters that Admiral Nimitz had when he moved out to Guam?

Admiral Pownall: Yes. They are not the ones that are in that book.

Mrs. Pownall: They were practically destroyed in that last typhoon. They rebuilt them.

Q: The ones you occupied were destroyed?

Mrs. Pownall: Almost destroyed, so that they practically rebuilt them.

Admiral Pownall: One way to entertain out there was to play croquet. The young officers played.

Charles Hartman, who we saw today, came out there when he was captain of the transports.* I don't know whether he ever played croquet or not.

Mrs. Pownall: All the ships that came out, came to call on us.

Q: Did you say you flew your flag on the ship of which he

---
*Rear Admiral Charles C. Hartman, USN.

was the skipper, Admiral Hartman, the Randall?

Admiral Pownall: No, he wasn't the skipper of the Randall.

Mrs. Pownall: It was the other captain, the one that lives up in Rancho Santa Fe.

Q: Admiral Goodwin. I always associate the two of them, because he was chief of staff to Admiral Hartman.

Mrs. Pownall: They were both out there; Hartman was there, too. Goodwin was the one we came back with.

Q: These pictures that we've been looking at. When you left Guam, Captain Goodwin was the skipper of that ship?

Mrs. Pownall: Yes.

Q: That's interesting.

Mrs. Pownall: Charles also flew his flag on the [inaudible] when he made that inspection--when we went to Manila, through the Bonins, to Japan, and China.

Q: Do we have any more on Guam?

Mrs. Pownall: We were always having very interesting people out there, outside of the Army and Navy, and so forth.

We had the anthropologists from the University of Hawaii. They came out. They were all interested in those islands. A great group of them stayed in the big guest house, where we kept people that we didn't keep either in our house or the guest house. They brought out Sir Peter Buck. He's attached to the University of Hawaii, and he's an Amari. That's one of the tribes from Australia. He seemed like an old man. He got up and did the native dances and the native songs for us and for this group that we were entertaining. It was the most interesting thing in the world.

After he'd gone, we were told that he requested that he be made a citizen of the United States. He lived in Honolulu. And we wouldn't give it to him.

So the British made him an honorary citizen and knighted him, "Sir Peter Buck."

Isn't it funny the things that we won't do. He was a wonderful, great big, fine looking native.

Admiral Pownall: One thing I remember was when I was ordered out to Guam, Admiral Nimitz said, "Pownall, you're my friend. I'm going to give you my dog." And he did. He was a pit bull, but he was a mental case.

Q: The dog was? He'd been through the war maybe.

Admiral Pownall: He's go right through a screen door. The only person who could really handle him was Dan, our Filipino boy.

One time that he was all right was when he was out with the native people and with cattle. Finally, we put him in the hospital, just like a patient. He died, he was overbred.

Mrs. Pownall: Some friend in Honolulu, that had these very fine ones, gave this to Admiral Nimitz. It was supposed to be a very fine dog. It turned out that he was in-bred, just ruined. He was a beautiful looking dog. The one person he got along with was this Filipino, Dan. Dan could lead him around like a little sheep or something. With the rest of us, he'd just carry on terrible.

Q: He wasn't any pleasure to have.

Mrs. Pownall: We just couldn't take care of him at all. He went through screen doors and everything else.

Q: No pleasure to have an animal around that's destructive.

Before we stop the record, I want you to go back on some of the stories we talked about at noon. When you see them on the tape, if you want to clip them out and put them in at the right place, that's fine. You were telling me about the fog.

Admiral Pownall: That was on Charlie Belknap's ship, a destroyer. I had left the <u>Ammen</u> and went to the <u>Reid</u>.

Q: That would have been back about 1913.

Admiral Pownall: Yes, on Long Island Sound. We'd work on gunnery and all that sort of thing during the week around Fisher's Island, and so on. Then we'd have liberty. This one pier was not in the city of New York. Our skipper was pretty clever; he had a brother that lived down there, so we used to go down there.

We had just gotten these new recruits aboard. One was this great big lad right off the farm. It was foggy weather in the sound. He was on the bow as lookout. We hadn't had a chance to teach him the procedure in the language.

So we got this from him, "Hey, Cap, and his hand went up, "I smell hay."

Charlie Belknap was quick enough. He said, "If you smell hay, I'm going to anchor." We anchored. In the sound, you're not very far from land.

Q: But the next morning when the fog lifted, you were just heading for an alfalfa field, weren't you?

Admiral Pownall: That's right, but we anchored in time.

Another story about Long Island Sound was when we were up there with Gene Wilson and Guy Vaughn. We caught a lot of bluefish. Bluefish is very good, particularly if you have a Filipino boy to cook them on the beach. We came in to Fort Jefferson with a lot of bluefish tied up, as you do on boats.

People came down to the docks, "I can't believe it. Where did they get those fish?"

We said we got them out right near this lighthouse.

"Can't believe it."

That afternoon a lot of boats went out to get bluefish. We were just lucky.

Q: They didn't catch any?

Mrs. Pownall: They didn't catch any. Gene Wilson or Guy Vaughn heard this woman say, "Do you think they really caught them, or do you think they bought them?" They were all hung up when they came in and anchored. We all dug clams. We had that wonderful clam broth, and steamed clams, and these bluefish.

Admiral Pownall: Gene Wilson was with United Aircraft, and Guy Vaughn was with Curtiss-Wright, as president. They'd invite Mary and myself, and sometimes Louisa. We had a rule, though, no business when we're out fishing. Because they were two competitors. I wouldn't go if they did.

Q: You've certainly had an illustrious career. I feel as though I should say, both of you.

Mrs. Pownall: Mine was just tagging along.

Q: I don't think that's true, is it, Admiral?

Admiral Pownall: No.

Q: They say that any admiral who's successful, has been successful partly because he had a good helpmate.

Admiral Pownall: I think so, that's right.

Q: That would appear to be true in this case.

Admiral Pownall: Yes, indeed.

Mrs. Pownall: I certainly enjoyed it, no doubt about that. Nobody could have enjoyed it more than I did. It has been a marvelous experience.

Q: You've had a very wonderful life. It's nice to be able to say that. So many people criticize and complain.

You were going to tell me one other incident about how one of the bays on San Clemente Island got its name.

Admiral Pownall: That was when Whiting was exec of the <u>Saratoga</u>. We were getting new ensigns. We had the heads of departments standing out there picking out their ensigns. I picked out this lad because he had a pencil in his pocket.

Q: You figured if he had a pencil he at least knew how to write.

Admiral Pownall: Then we came out to the Pacific and operated off San Clemente and anchored.

Q: What did you pick him to be?

Admiral Pownall: Assistant navigator.

We used to come into this place and anchor. It didn't have a name, so we named it. I named it, "Soapy Lehman" for this youngster. I think it was on one map that the Coast and Geodetic Survey did afterwards. As far as we were concerned, it was Lehman's Cove.

Q: You took a woman off there who was ill?

Admiral Pownall: That was later, on the *Ranger*.

On the *Ranger* we operated out of there. It happened this time, we were exchanging messages with the beach. Our quartermaster read this message from the beach, "Please send doctor." So we sent Jesse Wright.*

It happened that this man's wife--he was the Coast and Geodetic Survey man who had charge of the island--was very sick. I was operating captain then. The only thing to do was to bring her aboard and take her to San Diego. There were no facilities out there, so we did.

Q: This was also off the lighthouse at San Clemente?

Admiral Pownall: It was a lighthouse but not a lightship.

Q: Well, I guess we're coming to the end of the tape.
   Thank you so much for a lovely weekend.

---

*Lieutenant (junior grade) Jesse G. Wright, MC, USN.

Index

to

Reminiscences of

Vice Admiral Charles A. Pownall

U.S. Navy (Retired)

Admiralty Islands
    As Commander Marianas and governor of Guam in the late 1940s, Pownall sent a team of American medical personnel to assist after a multi-injury truck accident in the Admiralties, 202

Ammen, USS (DD-35)
    Destroyer was dragged across the harbor in Newport, Rhode Island, during storm in 1913, 18; difficulty anchoring in fog in Long Island Sound, 212-213; crew gets plentiful bluefish catch in Long Island Sound, 213

Anderson, Admiral Edwin A., USN (USNA, 1882)
    As Commander in Chief Asiatic Fleet in 1923, dispatched the Huron (CA-9) to Japan to render assistance after a massive earthquake in early September, 47, 52

Andrews, Vice Admiral Adolphus, USN (USNA, 1901)
    As Commander Scouting Force in the late 1930s, had his flag in the Enterprise (CV-6), 97; as Commander North Atlantic Coastal Frontier and Commandant of the Third Naval District in 1941-42, concerned with German submarines off the East Coast, 106

Antisubmarine Warfare
    The Roe (DD-24) sank a German submarine off Brest in 1918, 31-32, 36; Pownall devised lighting system on U.S. destroyers to aid pilots in sinking German submarines, 106-109; U-85 sunk by the USS Roper (DD-147) in April 1942, 107

Arctic Operations
    Flight operations from the Ranger (CV-4) in the mid-1930s, 86-87

Army Air Corps, U.S.
    Navy's Bureau of Aeronautics shared engine developments with the Army in the early 1930s until it seemed apparent that the Army had designs on Navy Air, 81-83

Army Air Forces, U.S.
    Worked out deal with Navy to share B-24s during World War II, 121-123

Aviation Training
    Student pilot Pownall had mishap during gunnery practice in the mid-1920s, 64-65; Pownall angered Chief of Naval Operations Ernest J. King with his criticisms of naval flight training and pilot assignment during World War II, 127-129; aviation cadet programs set up in colleges during World War II, 163-164; survival training for student pilots, 164; carrier kept off Pensacola to qualify student pilots during World War II, 164-165; higher scholastic standard set toward end of World War II, 166

Badger, Lieutenant Commander Oscar C., USN (USNA, 1911)
    On the staff of Commander in Chief Asiatic Fleet in 1923, difficulties bringing fleet of trucks into Tokyo after September earthquake, 51

Barnes, Lieutenant Guy Carlton, USN (USNA, 1908)
    Commanding officer of the Roe (DD-24) tried to fix salted boilers during transatlantic crossing in 1917, but finally had to turn back to Boston, 27; transported American and British personnel from Japan after the 1923 earthquake, 50-51

Battenberg Cup
    Trophy for best race boat won by the Enterprise (CV-6) in the late 1930s, 97-98, 118-119; the New Mexico (BB-48) won the cup from the Enterprise, 119-120

Bayly, Vice Admiral Sir Lewis, RN
    Rode the USS Roe (DD-24) from Queenstown, Ireland, to Liverpool in 1918, 28-29; kept a small rug in front of his desk to position visiting officers, 29-30; sympathetic handling of U.S. naval officer who hit a rock, 30

Belknap, Lieutenant Charles, Jr., USN (USNA, 1903)
    As Pownall's commanding officer of the Ammen (DD-35) in 1914, sent the ensign to temporarily command the Reid, 19; handling of anchor in tricky waters of Long Island Sound, 212-213

Bemis, Lieutenant Commander Harold M., USN (USNA, 1907)
    Flustered by presence of women in London naval district office after being at sea during World War I, 36-37

Berrien, Captain Frank D., USN (USNA, 1900)
    As commanding officer of the Lexington (CV-2) in 1928, narrowly escaped injury when he walked through a turning propeller, 74-75

Bloch, Admiral Claude C., USN  (USNA, 1899)
    As Commander in Chief U.S. Fleet in the late 1930s, congratulated Pownall, skipper of the Enterprise (CV-6), for his carrier's success with boat races, 120

Bonin Islands
    The Pownalls toured the Bonins after World War II in the admiral's capacity as Commander Marianas and governor of Guam, 177; used by the Japanese as a coaling station during World War II, 177, 209

Boundy, Commander James W., SC, USN
    Supply officer provided Pownall with 150 pounds of grass seed to cover American graves on a Pacific island during World War II, 172

Brest, France
    The Roe (DD-24) sank a German submarine off Brest in 1918, 31-32, 36; poor condition of hospital in Brest during World War I, 35

Bristol, Captain Arthur L., Jr., USN  (USNA, 1906)
    As skipper of the Ranger (CV-4) in the mid-1930s, brought liquor aboard the carrier despite Prohibition, 87-88

B-24
    Deal worked out between Navy and Army Air Forces to share this bomber during World War II, 121-123

Buck, Sir Peter
    Amari tribesman was guest of the Pownalls in Guam in the mid-to-late 1940s, 210

Bureau of Aeronautics
    Development of aircraft engines in the early 1930s, 79-81; see also Naval Aviation

Burke, Captain Arleigh A., USN  (USNA, 1923)
    As chief of staff to Commander Task Force 58, Rear Admiral Mitscher, accompanied his boss on a visit to Pownall in Pearl Harbor, and brought along several Japanese prisoners, 157

Butler, Major General Smedley D., USMC
    Marine Corps hero of the 1910s and 1920s was a Quaker, 4-5

Camp Pendleton, California
    Navy B-24 crews trained here during World War II, 122-123

Carrier Division Three
    Admiral Chester Nimitz provided division commander Pownall the use of the Indiana (BB-58) in the Pacific in 1943, 130-131; at Marcus Island in September 1943, 131-133; units of division in 1943, 132, 134; at Tarawa, 134; at Mili, 135-137, 149; during the Gilberts campaign, 137-144; during Marshalls campaign, 145-149

Carrier Operations
    Pownall's philosophy on best use of carriers, 151-152, 155; see also USS Enterprise (CV-6); USS Guadalcanal (CVE-60); HMS Illustrious; USS Langley (CV-1); USS Lexington (CV-2); USS Lexington (CV-16); USS Liscome Bay (CVE-56); USS Ranger (CV-4); USS Saratoga (CV-3); USS Yorktown (CV-10)

Chapin, Captain Frederick L., USN (USNA, 1883)
    Commanding officer of the Missouri (BB-11) turned down junior officer Pownall's request for transfer to submarine duty in the early 1910s because the latter was a spotter, 15-16

China
    USS John D. Ford (DD-228) went through typhoon off the Shantung Peninsula in the early 1920s, 45; aide Pownall's clever way of getting a message through to his boss in Hankow in the mid-1920s, 53-54; the Pownall family's experiences in the mid-1920s, 54-62; Chinese fascination with soap, 60; severity of Chinese courts in the early 1920s, 60-61; the United States repaid war debts to China from World War II with excess materiel in the Marianas and Guam, 179-180

Churchill, Sir Winston
    During Prime Minister Churchill's visit to the United States in early 1942, Pownall charged with getting him from Norfolk to Washington, D.C., 110-114

Clark, Rear Admiral Charles E., USN (USNA, 1864)
    Mrs. Pownall played bridge with Admiral Clark when they were stationed in Washington, D.C., in the early 1920s, 40-41

Clark, Captain Joseph J., USN  (USNA, 1918)
    Pownall's recollections of Clark as commanding officer of Pownall's flagship, the Yorktown (CV-10), in 1943, 139-140

Cluverius, Commander Wat T., USN  (USNA, 1896)
    Executive officer of the Mississippi (BB-23) in 1910 was more than fair to Passed Midshipman Pownall when the latter let the band slip away on unauthorized leave in England, 9-10

Consolidated Vultee Aircraft Corporation
    Provided the Navy and Army Air Forces with B-24s during World War II, and trained initial crews, 121-123

Coontz, Admiral Robert E., USN  (USNA, 1885)
    As Chief of Naval Operations in the early 1920s, supported Vice Admiral Sims's effort to ward off deterioration of destroyers, 42

Craig, Brigadier General Edward A., USMC
    Warned Pownall's daughter about armed Japanese soldier stragglers in the northern part of Guam in the late 1940s, 184-185

Crommelin, Lieutenant Commander Charles L., USN  (USNA, 1931)
    As Commander Air Group Five in late 1943, begged Pownall to be allowed to lead scouting mission on Tarawa, where he was wounded, 136-137

Curtiss Wright
    Navy encouraged this aircraft engine manufacturer to make two-row radial engines in the early 1930s so that there would be competition with Pratt & Whitney, 80

Denfeld, Admiral Louis E., USN  (USNA, 1912)
    As Commander in Chief Pacific Fleet in 1947, visited Pownalls, and brought along author, John Marquand, 206

Dewey, Admiral of the Navy George, USN  (USNA, 1858)
    Pownall assigned to write an essay on Dewey in the early 1900s, which was his first introduction to the Navy, 1-2

Duke of York, HMS
    Carried Prime Minister Winston Churchill to Norfolk in early 1942, 110

Earthquake
    Pownall was dispatched to Japan in the Huron (CA-9) to render assistance after the September 1923 earthquake, 46-53

Engines--Aircraft
    Development of two-row radial airplane engines in the early 1930s, 79-80; jet engines originally deemed too dangerous in the mid-1910s, 80

Enterprise, USS (CV-6)
    Pownall approached by commissioning commanding officer of this carrier in 1938 about being his successor, 92-93; after yard workers at Norfolk sabotaged carrier in late 1930s, construction was completed by the Navy, 95-96; flag officers and staffs on board in the late 1930s, 95-97; boat races netted the Battenberg Cup for this carrier in San Francisco in 1939, 97-98, 118-119; preparations and readiness for World War II, 99, 103-104; Pownall congratulated when carrier won sail and boat races, 120

Fitch, Rear Admiral Aubrey W., USN  (USNA, 1906)
    As Commander Air South Pacific in 1942, was promised B-24 bombers for use at Guadalcanal, 122

Forrestal, James V.
    Pownall's friendship with the Secretary of the Navy in the mid-1940s, 94-95

Frost, Lieutenant Commander Holloway H., USN  (USNA, 1910)
    While at the Naval War College in the early 1920s, dictated that a destroyer had to be within 500 yards to sink a large ship, 46

Geiger, Major General Roy S., USMC
    Visited Pensacola for some much-needed rest toward the end of World War II, 165

German Navy
    Commander North Atlantic Coastal Frontier, Rear Admiral Adolphus Andrews, was concerned about threat of German submarines sinking U.S. tankers off the East Coast in 1941-42, 106; 29 Germans buried in Virginia after the USS Roper (DD-147) sank the U-85 in April 1942, 107

Gilbert Islands Campaign
    Successful use of fighter direction by carriers in late 1943, 138; Commander Carrier Division Three Pownall decorated by British for his part in this campaign, 138, 143-144; see also Tarawa

Gleaves, Rear Admiral Albert, USN (USNA, 1877)
    As Commander Atlantic Fleet Cruiser and Transport Force in 1917 ordered towline to the Roe (DD-24) cut and ordered her back to the United States, 27

Griffin, Lieutenant Commander Virgil C., Jr., USN (USNA, 1912)
    Difficulties as air officer in the Lexington (CV-2) in the late 1920s, 74

Guadalcanal
    Commander Air South Pacific, Rear Admiral Fitch, was promised--and received--B-24 bombers for use at Guadalcanal in 1942, 122

Guadalcanal, USS (CVE-60)
    Larger carrier used for pilot training in response to Pownall's suggestion during World War II, 129

Guam
    Pownall's duties as naval governor of Guam from 1946 to 1949, 173-174, 188-200; Pownall insisted that only Guamanians be allowed to conduct business immediately after the war, 174, 200-201; three services maintained bases on Guam after the war, 176; President Harry Truman reestablished civil law on Guam, 177-178; Admiral Chester Nimitz let Pownall decide whether dependents would be allowed on Guam, 180-181; Pownall allowed the Marines low-keyed gambling to raise welfare funds, even though Guam law forbade it, 181; relations with Japanese during World War II, 182-183, 201; straggling Japanese soldiers killed American soldiers after Japanese surrender, 183-186; Pownall received citation in 1948 from the bishop of Guam, 187-188; question of self-government studied, 188-189; Pownall's relationship with Guam congress, 188-190, 193-194; question of sending American war dead home from Guam cemeteries, 190-191; language and education, 194-195; Americans arranged for cattle and chickens for the island, 198-199; Pownall injured in bridge collapse, 203-204; Pownalls hosted many influential visitors, 190-191, 195-198, 204-206, 210; social life, 207-208

Guantanamo, Cuba
    Bluejackets from the Missouri (BB-11) were ordered ashore in June 1912 to retake a Guantanamo sugar mill captured by Cubans, 16-18

Halligan, Lieutenant Commander John, Jr., USN (USNA, 1898)
    Facetious comment about surfeit of medals given out by the French during World War I, 34

Hughes, Rear Admiral Charles F., USN (USNA, 1888)
    During the early 1920s, the Pownalls lived in Admiral Hughes's Washington, D.C., apartment, complete with his furniture, 39-41

Huron, USS (CA-9)
    Near collision with the John D. Ford (DD-228) off Java in the early 1920s, 46; sent to Japan to render assistance after the September 1923 earthquake, 46-53

Idaho, USS (BB-24)
    Race boat stolen by archrival Mississippi (BB-23) crew in 1910, 12-14

Illustrious, HMS
    While in Norfolk for repairs in 1942, the commanding officer of this British carrier was forced to wear the only uniform not lost when the carrier was damaged--shorts, 117-118

Indiana, USS (BB-58)
    This battleship was assigned to Task Force 50 in late 1943 to offer extra assistance, 130-131

Indianapolis, USS (CA-35)
    When Pownall rode in this cruiser with his boss, Admiral Raymond Spruance, in 1944, he found a creative way to direct Pacific air operations despite radio silence, 155, 158

Iowa, USS (BB-61)
    Japanese cruiser at Truk fired a torpedo at this battleship at Truk in 1944 to test its range, 159

Iowa State University
    The Navy set up an aviation cadet program here during World War II to overcome shortage of pilots, 163-164

Japan
>USS Huron (CA-9) dispatched from China to Japan immediately after the September 1923 earthquake, 46-53; American difficulties with Japanese soldier stragglers on isolated Pacific islands who didn't know that the war was over, 183-186

John D. Ford, USS (DD-228)
>Operations in the early 1920s, 44-46; near-miss with another cruiser off Java, 46

King, Admiral Ernest J., USN (USNA, 1914)
>As an older student aviator in the mid-1920s, asked his friend Pownall's advice on taking a stunt pilot course, 65-66; assessed as Commander Aircraft Base Force in the mid-1930s by his chief of staff, Pownall, 89; all of King's baggage was lost in a patrol plane mishap near Acapulco in the mid-1930s, 89-90; as Commander in Chief U.S. Fleet in 1942, ordered secrecy about successful antisubmarine aid devised by Pownall in 1942, 109; supported Pownall's decision to provide transportation for Lord Louis Mountbatten from Norfolk to New York in 1942, 117; attended party at Pownall's San Diego quarters in the early 1940s, 125-126; angered by Pownall's criticisms of naval flight training and pilot assignment, 127-129; critical of Commander Carrier Division Three Pownall's failure to follow up at Kwajalein with a second attack, 147-148

Kobayashi, Rear Admiral Seizo, IJN
>Friendly towards U.S. Navy personnel offering assistance during 1923 Japanese earthquake, 48

Kusaw
>Native chief pledged allegiance to the United States after World War II, 182

Kwajalein
>Commander Task Force 50 Pownall criticized for lack of aggressiveness at Kwajalein in late 1943, 147-148

Langley, USS (CV-1)
>Anecdote about meeting of Langley and Ranger (CV-4) at San Diego in the mid-1930s, 87

Lee, Rear Admiral Willis A., Jr., USN (USNA, 1908)
>Pownall's comment to Lee, Commander Battleships Pacific and Commander Task Group 50.8, before the Marshalls campaign in late 1943, 146

Leighton, Lieutenant Commander Bruce G., USN  (USNA, 1913)
    Involved in test aircraft bombing of battleships in the
    early 1930s, 83

Lexington, USS (CV-2)
    Knocked down lampposts while transiting the Panama Canal
    in 1927, 71; ineffective chain of command organization
    changed by Pownall in 1928, 73-74

Lexington, USS (CV-16)
    Pownall would have preferred this new carrier as his
    flagship when he became Commander Carrier Division Three
    in 1943, 130; Pownall moved his flag on board for second
    strike on Tarawa in late 1943, 135; brought aboard plane
    with dangerously low fuel level after the Liscome Bay
    (CVE-56) was sunk in November 1943, 140; Pownall blames
    torpedo this carrier took at Kwajalein on lack of
    support from escorting cruiser, 140; poor quality of
    flag quarters on board, 152

Liberty
    The band of the Mississippi (BB-23) fooled junior
    officer Pownall into letting them go on unauthorized
    leave in England in 1910, 8-10

Liscome Bay, USS (CVE-56)
    USS Yorktown (CV-10) took on some of the Liscome Bay's
    planes after the carrier was sunk in November 1943, 139

Lockwood, Vice Admiral Charles A., Jr., USN  (USNA, 1912)
    As Commander Submarines Pacific Fleet in 1943,
    approached by Pownall about the possibility of using
    submarines to pick up downed pilots, 131

Long Island Sound
    USS Ammen (DD-35)'s difficulties anchoring in fog in the
    early 1910s, 212-213; good bluefish catch off the
    lighthouse, 213

MacArthur, General Douglas, USA  (USMA, 1903)
    After World War II, wanted senior command of the entire
    Pacific area, but the Joint Chiefs of Staff thought that
    was too much power for one man, 175; senior officer in
    charge of the Marianas in the mid-to-late 1940s, 175;
    took lone Japanese sympathizer in Guam off Pownall's
    hands after World War II, 183

McCabe, Thomas B.
    As Foreign Liquidation Commissioner and Special
    Assistant to the Secretary of State after World War II,
    used ingenuity in arranging to repay war debts to China
    with unwanted materiel in the Marianas and Guam, 179-180

McCormick, Colonel Robert
    *Chicago Tribune* editor visited Guam in the late 1940s,
    195-198

McKittrick, Lieutenant Harold V., USN  (USNA, 1907)
    Dealt with kindly by a British admiral after his ship
    hit a rock during World War I, 30

McMorris, Rear Admiral Charles H., USN  (USNA, 1912)
    As member of Admiral Nimitz's Pacific Fleet staff, had a
    hand in Pownall's citation after his September 1943
    Marcus Island success, 134

McVay, Rear Admiral Charles B., Jr., USN  (USNA, 1890)
    As Commander Yangtze River Patrol in the mid-1920s,
    received a message using an admiral's personal code
    number while he was dining with that admiral, 54

Marcus Island
    Task Force 50's successful attack against
    Marcus in September 1943, 131-133

Mariana Islands
    Pownall's duties as Commander Marianas from 1946 to
    1949, 170, 176; Pownall provided belly tanks to the
    natives in 1946 for use in catching rain water, 170;
    General MacArthur given control over the Marianas in the
    mid-to-late 1940s, 175; unified command of the Marianas
    and Guam kept by the Navy in the post-War period, 175-
    176, 178

Marine Corps, U.S.
    Diffculties of Marines at Tarawa caused by extensive use
    of pillboxes by the Japanese, 134; Guam governor Pownall
    allowed Marines to keep low-key gambling on the island
    after World War II, despite civil law forbidding it,
    181; even after Japanese surrender,
    Japanese stragglers killed a number of Marines on Guam,
    183-186

Marshall Islands
   Commander Task Force 50 Pownall concerned about his division's participation in this campaign in late 1943, because he knew that his pilots were worn out from action in the Gilberts, 145-147; Pownall attributes difficulties in the Marshalls to American planes loaded with torpedoes instead of bombs, 146

Medicine
   Medical research at the Pensacola Naval Air Station toward the end of World War II, 166; Americans provided medical assistance throughout the isolated Pacific islands in the mid-to-late 1940s, 170, 202-203

Merrill, Midshipman Robert T. II, USN (USNA, 1910)
   Threw mince pie in Midshipman Pownall's face during argument, 7

Mili
   Task Force 50 tasked with controlling this island during Gilberts campaign in late 1943, 135-137, Pownall resorted to impromptu signal to American submarine to rescue a plane that had crash-dived alongside, 149-150

Mississippi, USS (BB-23)
   This battleship's band took advantage of junior officer Pownall's inexperience to talk their way into unauthorized leave during visit to England in 1910, 8-10; crew stole raceboat from archrival Idaho (BB-24), 12-14

Missouri, USS (BB-11)
   As junior officer in this battleship in the early 1910s Pownall put in for submarine duty, but was turned down because he was a spotter, 15-16; a contingent of the crew was sent ashore in June 1912 to retake a Guantanamo sugar mill that had been captured by Cubans, 16-18

Mitscher, Vice Admiral Marc A., USN (USNA, 1910)
   As Commander Task Force 58 in 1944, working relationship with Commander Fifth Fleet Raymond A. Spruance, 155; relieved Pownall as Commander Carrier Division Three in 1944, 156-157; visited Pownall in Pearl Harbor in 1944, and brought along several Japanese prisoners, 157; made strike on Truk and Saipan in 1944, 160; visited Pensacola for some much-needed rest, 164-165

Moffett, Rear Admiral William A., USN  (USNA, 1890)
Assessed as Chief of the Bureau of Aeronautics in the early 1930s, 81; initially encouraged sharing engine development information with the Army, 81-82

Molten, Lieutenant Commander Robert P., Jr., USN  (USNA, 1911)
Difficulties as air officer in Lexington (CV-2) in the late 1920s, 74

Moore, Captain Charles J., USN  (USNA, 1910)
As Admiral Raymond A. Spruance's chief of staff in 1944, presented suggestion that Truk be bypassed that was quickly accepted up the chain of command, 158-159

Mountbatten, Captain Louis, RN
Pownall arranged for Lord Mountbatten to be flown by an American pilot from Norfolk to New York in 1942, even though there had been a directive against taxiing the British around, 116-117; saw the Battenberg Cup, named after his grandfather, when he visited the West Virginia (BB-48) during World War II, 119-120

Murray, Rear Admiral George D., USN  (USNA, 1911)
Speculation that Pownall's predecesor as naval governor of Guam ran into trouble with bishop of Guam, 166-167; advised Pownall on loyalty of Guamanians, 183

Naval Air Training Command
Missions of air stations Pownall was in charge of in 1944-1945, 160; officers on Pownall's staff, 160-161; see also Aviaiton Training

Naval Aviation
Difficulty recruiting enough pilots in the mid-to-late 1930s, 78-79; Arctic flight operations off the Ranger (CV-4) in the mid-1930s, 86-87; British pilots, trained at Norfolk during World War II, were forced to reverse landing signals to conform to U.S. signals, 115-116; successful use of fighter direction during Gilberts campaign in 1943, 138; see also Aviation Training; Bureau of Aeronautics; Night Flying; Patrol Planes; Naval Air Training Command

Naval Academy, U.S.
Pownall fenced as a midshipman prior to graduation in 1910, 6; Pownall's writeup in class of 1910 Lucky Bag, 6-7

Naval Forces Europe
    Pownall's recollections from service on the staff of Commander Naval Forces Europe, Vice Admiral William Sims, in 1918-19, 36-37

Neutrality Patrol
    The *Reid* patrolled off Boston in the mid-1910s, 25-26

New Jersey, USS (BB-62)
    Pownall occupied the captain's daytime quarters in this battleship in 1944, 158

Night Flying
    Pownall pioneered idea of putting vertical red lights on destroyers to assist Navy pilots during night antisubmarine operations in the early 1940s, 106-109

Nimitz, Fleet Admiral Chester W., USN  (USNA, 1905)
    Tried to recruit Pownall to submarine duty in the early 1910s, 15; friendship with Pownall, 94-95; encouraged Pownall to move his Fleet Air, West Coast command from San Diego to San Francisco during World War II, but was turned down, 123-124; involved in patrol plane accident in June 1942, 124; almost caught the mumps at party at Pownall's quarters, 125-126; assigned Pownall as Commander Carrier Division Three in 1943, and gave him the use of battleships, 130-131; commended Pownall for performance at Marcus Island in September 1943, 133; Pownall told Nimitz of inside details about Kwajalein difficulties, 148; removed profane message that Pownall used on the spur of the moment from signal book, 150-151; discouraged Pownall from turning the Marianas command over to the Air Force in the mid-to-late 1940s, 175; allowed Pownall to decide whether dependents would be allowed on Guam, 180; gave Pownall his pit bull before he left Guam, 210-211

Norfolk Naval Air Station
    Complimented by Prime Minister Winston Churchill during visit in early 1942, 111; collision of U.S. and British planes while taxiing in early 1940s, 115; British pilots were trained at Norfolk during World War II, 115-116

Norfolk Navy Yard
    Sabotage on carrier *Enterprise* (CV-6) at shipyard in the late 1930s, 95-96; repair base for Allied carriers during World War II, 114-115, 117-118

North Carolina, University of
   The Navy set up an aviation cadet program here during
   World War II to overcome shortage of pilots, 163-164

Nulton, Admiral Louis M., USN  (USNA, 1889)
   As Commander in Chief Battle Fleet in the late 1920s,
   dislike of aviation and the Marines, 76-77; assessed by
   Pownall, 77

Palau Islands
   As Commander Marianas in 1946, Pownall's recollections
   of the Palaus, 171; troubles with Japanese stragglers
   after the War who didn't know about the surrender, 184

Patrol Planes
   Admiral Ernest King's baggage lost in patrol plane
   sinking off Acapulco in the mid-1930s, 89-90; Pownall
   sees Navy's purchase of B-24s during World War II as
   beginning of the end for Navy's patrol planes, 121-123

Pearl Harbor
   The Pownalls' recollections of 7 December 1941, 105

Pearson, Drew
   Muckraking columnist suggested that Admiral Marc
   Mitscher, General Roy Geiger, and Pownall were wasting
   government funds with a fishing trip during World War
   II, 165

PB2Y Coronado
   Trials in California in 1942, 121

Penmarch, France
   High fatality rate during escort duty off Penmarch
   during World War I, 31

Pensacola Naval Air Station
   "Ghost" roamed Quarters A, where the Pownall's lived in
   1944-1945, 161-163; see also Naval Air Training Command

Philippines
   Pownall believed that the Japanese would attack the
   Philippines, instead of Pearl Harbor in late 1941, 105

Pownall, Vice Admiral Charles A., USN  (USNA, 1910)
   Birth in 1887 and early education, 1-2; parents, 2-3;
   citations and awards, 133, 138, 142-144, 168-169;
   midshipman at Naval Academy, 1906-1910, 3, 6-8; duty in
   the Mississippi (BB-23) in the early 1910s, 8-14; duty
   in the Missouri (BB-11) in the early 1910s, 15-18; duty

in the Ammen (DD-35) in the early 1910s, 18-19, 212-214; commanding officer of the Reid (DD-21) 1914-1915, 19-26; postgraduate studies in Annapolis and New York, 25-26; executive and commanding officer of the Roe (DD-24) and commanding officer of the Vedette (SP-163) from 1917-1918, 26-36; aide to Commander Naval Forces Europe, 1918-1919, 31, 36-38; duty in the Material Division, Office of the Chief of Naval Operations, 1919-1921, 38-43; commanding officer, USS John D. Ford (DD-228), from 1921 to 1923, 41, 44-46; duty on the staff of Commander in Chief Asiatic Fleet, 1923-1924, 46-62; duty in the Ship Repair Division of the Bureau of Engineering, from 1924 to 1925, 62-63; aide to Assistant Secretary of the Navy Robinson from 1925-1926, 63; flight training at Pensacola from 1926-1927, 63-66; navigator in Saratoga (CV-3) from 1927 to 1928, 55-56, 66-73, 215-216; air officer in the Lexington (CV-2) from 1928 to 1929, 73-76; aviation officer on staff of Commander Battle Force from 1929 to 1930, 76-77; head of the Power Plant and Experimental Section, Bureau of Aeronautics, 1930 to 1933, 79-83; executive officer, USS Ranger (CV-4) from 1934 to 1936, 84-88, 216; chief of staff to Commander Aircraft Base Force from 1936 to 1937, 88-91; head of the flight division, Bureau of Aeronautics, 1937 to 1938, 78-79, 91-92; commanding officer of the Enterprise (CV-6), 1938 to 1941, 57-58, 92-104, 118-120; Commander Naval Air Station, Naval Operating Base, Norfolk, from 1941 to 1942, 104-118, 120; Commander Patrol Plane Replacement Squadrons, Patrol Wings, Pacific Fleet and Commander Fleet Air West Coast from 1942 to 1943, 120-129; Commander Carrier Division Three from 1943 to 1944, 130-154; Commander Air Force Pacific Fleet, February to September 1944, 154-160; Chief of Naval Air Training Command from 1944 to 1945, 129, 160-169; Commander Marianas and naval governor of Guam from 1946 to 1949, 169-211

Pownall, Louisa
See Wagner, Louisa Pownall

Pownall, Mary Chenoweth
Dated her future husband while he was a midshipman prior to graduation in 1910, 3, 6; played bridge with Rear Admiral Charles Clarke in Washington in the early 1920s, 40-41; confronted with possibility that her husband's ship was lost in a typhoon in the early 1920s, 45; experiences in China in the early 1920s, 55-62; entertained husband's fellow flight students in the mid-

1920s, 66; furnished whiskey to her husband on board the Ranger (CV-4) in the mid-1930s for medicinal purposes, 87; recollections as First Lady of Guam from 1946 to 1949, 171, 173-174, 178-189, 195-197, 199-201, 204-205, 207-211

Pratt & Whitney
Made two-row radial aircraft engines for the Navy in the early 1930s, 80-81

Pratt, Brigadier General Henry Conger, USA (USMA, 1904)
Anecdote about General Pratt as Assistant Chief of the Army Air Corps in the early 1930s, 82

Prohibition
USS Ranger (CV-4) crew brought liquor aboard the carrier for medicinal purposes in the mid-1930s despite Prohibition, 87-88

Ranger, USS (CV-4)
Tonnage adjusted to carrier's disadvantage to adhere to 1930 London Naval Conference standards, 84-86; winter flight operations in the mid-1930s, 86-87; brought medical assistance to a woman on San Clemente Island in the mid-1930s, 216

Read, Captain Albert C., USN (USNA, 1907)
As Chief of Naval Air Training in the 1930s, tried unsuccessfully to uncover source of mysterious noises in Quarters A at Pensacola, 162

Reeves, Rear Admiral Joseph M., USN (USNA, 1894)
As Commander Aircraft Squadrons Battle Fleet in 1928, supported Pownall's request to change the change of command in the USS Lexington (CV-2) to a more conventional organization, 74

Reid, USS (DD-21)
The Reid's commanding officer was replaced on the spot at Veracruz in 1914 during an inspection by Commander Atlantic Destroyer Flotilla, and drunken crew members were removed, 18-19; Ensign Pownall was put in temporary command, 19-21; terrible condition of ship, 21; Pownall criticized for Reid's salted bottom at Veracruz, 22; difficulties in fireroom nearly resulted in tragedy, 23-24; neutrality patrol off Boston in 1914, 25

Religion
> Pownall's handling of potential conflicts of military service and his Quaker beliefs, 4-5; missionaries in the Marianas after World War II, 182; Pownall received citation from the bishop of Guam in 1948, 187-188

Richardson, Admiral James O., USN (USNA, 1902)
> As Chief of the Bureau of Navigation in 1938, approved selection of Pownall as commanding officer of the Enterprise (CV-6), 92-93; as Commander Battle Force, riding in the Enterprise in 1939, had crew man antiaircraft batteries twice a day, 99; relieved after expressing disapproval over massing of U.S. fleet at Pearl Harbor in 1941, 99-101; assessed by Pownall, 100-102

Richardson, Mrs. James O.
> Wife of Commander South China Patrol evacuated from Tokyo after the 1923 earthquake, 50; stayed with Mrs. Pownall in 1941, 100

Roe, USS (DD-24)
> Salted boilers responsible for aborted transatlantic crossing in the fall of 1917, 27; difficulties retaining oil, 28; former executive officer Pownall returned in mid-1918 as skipper when the commanding officer took ill, 28; carried British admiral from Queenstown, Ireland, to Liverpool, 28-29; torpedoed German submarine off Brest in 1918, 31-32, 36; rescued crews from torpedoed ships, 33-34

Roper, USS (DD-147)
> Sank the German U-85 in April 1942, 107; captain received Navy Cross for U-85 sinking, 109

Royal Navy
> British aircraft carriers were repaired at Norfolk during World War II, 114-115, 117-118; Royal Navy pilots trained at Norfolk Naval Air Station during World War II, 115-116; aee also Captain Louis Mountbatten, RN

St. Mary's College (San Francisco, California)
> The Navy set up an aviation cadet program here during World War II to overcome shortage of pilots, 163-164, 168

Saltonstall, Senator Leverett (Republican-Massachusetts)
> Went to Guam in the late 1940s with the intention of removing his son's body back to the United States, but changed his mind, 190-191

San Clemente Island, California
   Pownall named a bay off San Clemente Island after his assistant navigator in the Saratoga (CV-3) in the late 1920s, and the name--Lehman's Cove--is now on some official maps, 215-216

San Diego, USS (CL-53)
   Fired upon accidently at Mili in late 1943 by American ships trying to hit a Japanese plane, 153

San Francisco, California
   The Enterprise (CV-6)'s race boat won a competition at San Francisco exposition in 1939, 97-98

Saratoga, USS (CV-3)
   High morale in carrier in late 1920s, 66, 69; original crew in 1927, 67, 69-70; nearly ran aground during initial trip from Camden to Philadelphia, 67-69; examples of Pownall's skill as navigator, 67-68, 71; short skipper had bridge rail lowered, 72; Pownall piloted the carrier into Bremerton without the benefit of his just-broken Fathometer, 72-73

Sherman, Rear Admiral Frederick C., USN  (USNA, 1910)
   As Commander Task Group 50.4 during the Marshalls campaign in late 1943, dealings with Commander Task Force 50 Pownall, 146

Sims, Vice Admiral William S., USN  (USNA, 1880)
   As commanding officer of the Minnesota (BB-22), Commander Sims greatly improved naval gunnery techniques in the early 1910s, 10-11; made a stirring speech to American and British naval officers at Gravesend, England, in 1910 that resulted in his removal from command, 11-12; as Commander Atlantic Destroyer Flotilla in 1914, removed commanding officer of the Reid (DD-21) on the spot during a particularly poor inspection in 1914, 18-19; returned Pownall's call on board the Reid, 23; as Commander U.S. Naval Forces Operating in European Waters, kept destroyer Roe (DD-24) in France during World War I despite her difficulties retaining oil, 28; invited Pownall to attend Queenstown Association social function, 29; concerned about deterioration of destroyers after World War I, 42-43

Spruance, Vice Admiral Raymond A., USN  (USNA, 1907)
   As Commander Fifth Fleet in 1944, Pownall's boss, 155, 158

Stump, Captain Felix B., USN  (USNA, 1917)
    As Commander Carrier Division Three from 1943 to 1944, Pownall wanted Stump's ship, the <u>Lexington</u> (CV-16), as his flagship, 130; coordinated landing of pilot who was dangerously low of fuel, 140; apologized to Pownall for condition of flag quarters in the <u>Lexington</u>, 152

Submarines
    Commander North Atlantic Coastal Frontier, Vice Admiral Adolphus Andrews, concerned about German submarines off the East Coast in 1941-1942, 106; Commander Carrier Division Three Pownall's suggestion of using submarines to rescue downed pilots in 1943 led to more than 500 rescues, 131, 149-151

Swift, Major General Innis P., USA  (USMA, 1904)
    As Commanding General, First Cavalry Division during World War II, asked Pownall for grass seed to use to cover American graves on a Pacific island, 171-172

Taffinder, Captain Sherwoode A., USN  (USNA, 1906)
    Pownall's relationship with Taffinder, who was chief of staff to Admiral J.O. Richardson in early 1940s, 102-103

Taft, William Howard
    President Taft ordered bluejackets from the <u>Missouri</u> (BB-11) ashore in 1912 to retake a Cuban sugar mill, 16-18

Tarawa
    Difficulties for U.S. Marines caused by extensive use of Japanese pillboxes, 134; phosphorus bomb on Task Force 50 unit almost gave away division approach on Tarawa in late 1943, 135; air group commander injured during scouting raid on island, 136-137

Towers, Vice Admiral John H., USN  (USNA, 1906)
    As Commander Air Force Pacific Fleet in late 1943, critical of Commander Carrier Division Three Pownall for his failure to follow up with a second attack at Kwajalein, 147-148; annoyed at rule that only Guamanians could conduct business in Guam immediately after World War II, 174, 200-201

Truk Island
    Captain Charles Moore, Admiral Spruance's chief of staff, convinced the powers that be to bypass Truk in 1944, 158-159

Truman, Harry S.
   President Truman reestablished civil laws on Guam after
   World War II, 177

Typhoon
   USS John D. Ford (DD-228) went through a typhoon off the
   Shantung Peninsula in the early 1920s, 45

U-85 (German Submarine)
   Sunk off the Virginia coast by the USS Roper (DD-147) in
   April 1942, 107

Ulithi
   As Commander Marianas in 1946, Pownall was impressed
   with the honesty of Ulithi natives, 170-171

Vedette, USS (SP-163)
   Just adequate for convoy duty off the French coast
   during World War I because she was not much faster than
   the ships she was escorting, 28, former yacht of
   financier Frederick Vanderbilt, 31; returned to
   Vanderbilt after the war, 38-39

Veracruz, Mexico
   Ensign Pownall put in command of the Reid (DD-21) at
   Veracruz in 1914, 19-21; Pownall's experiences at
   Veracruz, 22

Wagner, Louisa Pownall
   Experiences in China in the mid-1920s, 55, 61-62;
   contracted the measles in Baguio, 56-57; as dependent in
   Guam after World War II, 181, 184-185

Washington, Admiral Thomas, USN  (USNA, 1887)
   As Commander in Chief Asiatic Fleet in the mid-1920s,
   anecdote concerning aide Pownall's use of this
   communications code, 53-54

West Virginia, USS (BB-48)
   Won the Battenberg Cup away from the Enterprise (CV-6)
   in the early 1940s, 119-120

White, Captain Newton H., Jr., USN  (USNA, 1907)
   First Enterprise (CV-6) skipper in 1938 approached
   Pownall about being his successor, 92-93

Whiting, Commander Kenneth, USN  (USNA, 1905)
   Assessed as executive officer of the USS Saratoga (CV-3)
   in the late 1920s, 69-70; accidently broke Saratoga's
   Fathometer, 72

Wiltse, Rear Admiral Lloyd Jerome, USN  (USNA, 1914)
   As Commander Cruiser Division Two in late 1943 at Mili, sent message to let American ships in area know that they were accidently firing on his flagship, the San Diego (CL-53), 153

Woolsey, Commodore W.B., USN
   Ghost of Woolsey, first officer to occupy Quarters A at Pensacola in 1874, supposedly still in house, 161-163

Wright, Rear Admiral Carleton H., USN  (USNA, 1912)
   Duties as Deputy High Commissioner of the Pacific Trust Territories in 1946, 170

Wright, Lieutenant Jerauld, USN  (USNA, 1918)
   As executive officer of the John D. Brown (DD-228) in the early 1920s, his ship was ordered into Manila so he could visit his father, the commanding general of the Philippines, who was ill, 45

Wright, Lieutenant (junior grade) Jesse G., MC, USN
   Medical officer in the Ranger (CV-4) assisted a sick woman on San Clemente Island in the mid-1930s, 216

Yap Island
   As Commander Marianas in 1946, Pownall's recollections of Yap, 171

Yarnell, Captain Harry E., USN  (USNA, 1897)
   Saratoga (CV-3) skipper came to respect navigator Pownall's knowledge of currents and tides in 1927, 67-68; had Saratoga bridge rail lowered so that he could see over it, 72; parting advice to Pownall about refusing certain orders, 73

Yorktown, USS (CV-10)
   Served as Commander Task Force 50's flagship for Marcus Island and Tarawa assaults in late 1943, 130-134; took on some of the Liscome Bay (CVE-56)'s planes after that carrier was sunk in November 1943, 139; funeral on board in, 140; mess attendant acted as chaplain, 140-141; won Presidential Unit Citation, 141-142; American plane crash-landed in water near this carrier, 149-151, 153; poor quality of flag quarters on board, 152; bridge grazed by Japanese bullet, 152

www.ingramcontent.com/pod-product-compliance
Lightning Source LLC
Chambersburg PA
CBHW080614170426
43209CB00007B/1434